THE FEMININE FIX-IT
AUTO HANDBOOK

Also by Kay B. Ward
THE FEMININE FIX-IT HANDBOOK

THE FEMININE FIX-IT AUTO HANDBOOK

Written and Illustrated by
Kay B. Ward

GROSSET & DUNLAP
Publishers • New York

Published simultaneously in Canada
Library of Congress catalog card number: 73–15126
ISBN 0–448–01033–X

First printing

Printed in the United States of America

To my father, who taught me what a lug wrench was

CONTENTS

INTRODUCTION

FACE IT! IF you're reading this book, you're about to become a deeper part of that American fantasy, that overindulged or badly neglected hunk of metal, that dream machine, the automobile.

Right at the beginning, let me tell you that this is *not* an auto repair book. If you're really interested in auto mechanics, there are any number of books on the market on this subject, from simple guides to technical, illustrated manuals. This book, as it is titled, is a handbook.

It is divided roughly into three sections: the first twelve chapters deal with mechanical aspects of your car: fuel, lubrication, brakes, suspension and so on; the next four discuss general driving problems: choosing a car, rules and regulations, emergencies, insurance, and so forth. The final chapter is a comprehensive "Trouble Chart" of common car problems— and their likely causes.

Don't let anyone try to convince you that in order to know about the workings of a car you must be able to repair it yourself. The first portion of this book will prove to you that you can go far on theoretical understanding. For instance, you'll have some idea of what that protesting squawk from the rear wheel means, and you'll be able to explain the problem intelligently to your mechanic. You'll know the difference between the water pump and the fuel pump, the alternator and the crankshaft, the wheel bearings and the brake shoes. You'll learn the parts involved in the fuel system, the cooling system, and the lubricating system, and how they function, so that when your mechanic talks to you about the distributor or the coil, you'll know what he is speaking about.

As far as actual repairs go, this book *will* tell you in detail how to change a tire, how to cable-jump a battery, and how to make minor body repairs. The tools you'll need for these repairs are ones that every driver should carry in her kit. They're described in detail in Chapter 1.

To get you started, here's the basic theory of the internal combustion system, which employs the standard U.S. gasoline engine. The diagram below shows many components of the system, all of which are later described and illustrated in detail.

1. Fuel is pumped by the fuel pump to the carburetor.
2. The carburetor converts this fuel to a vapor by combining it with air. This vapor is passed through the intake manifold and forced into the cylinder holes.
3. The electrical ignition, when activated, causes the spark plugs mounted over the cylinder holes to spark, thus causing a small explosion in each fuel-vapor-filled cylinder hole.
4. This explosion forces the pistons inside the cylinders to be pressed downward in sequence. A valve arrangement above each cylinder controls the amount of vapor that goes into the cylinders.

5. As the spark plugs keep sparking and the fuel vapor continues its controlled flow, these explosions continue, keeping the pistons moving up and down and the engine running—pam, pam, pam, pam, with each explosion.
6. Attached to the end of each piston is a piston rod, and linked through this rod is the crankshaft. The explosions causing the pistons to go up and down rotate this crankshaft.
7. Attached, in front, to the crankshaft are timing gears, fan belt, and cooling fan, and at the rear of the crankshaft a flywheel (or driveplate, in cars with automatic transmissions).
8. The flywheel (or driveplate) regulates and controls the spinning crankshaft and transmits this controlled rotation to the transmission.
9. The transmission, in turn, transmits this rotating movement to the wheels.
10. Wastes from combustion are passed out through the exhaust manifold through the exhaust system and out the tailpipe.

Now you're ready to roll. This is your handbook for better auto maintenance and driving—keep it nearby for quick reference.

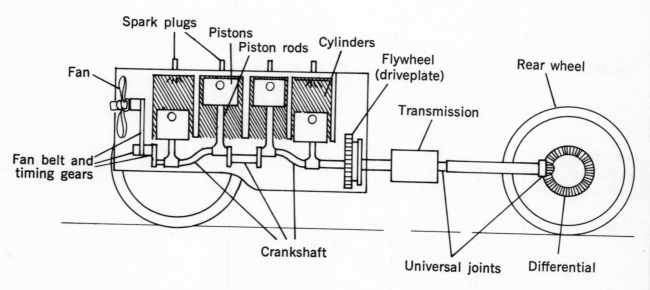

THE FEMININE FIX-IT
AUTO HANDBOOK

1. SOME USEFUL TOOLS FOR YOUR CAR

You may never need any of these tools—but having them available could make the difference between continuing on your way or being stranded for hours.

THE JACK

I'm sure you've already come in contact with this tool, since all of us who drive have at one time or another experienced a flat tire. These are the three kinds of jack commonly used:

1. *The axle jack.* This type of jack is inserted under the axle of the car. As the jack is cranked upward, the car is raised at the axle.

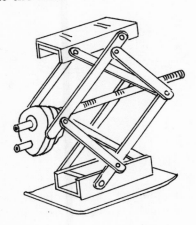

2. *The bumper jack.* As you might guess, this jack locks underneath the bumper and, as it is raised, lifts the car by the bumper. Most U.S. manufacturers supply bumper jacks with their new cars.

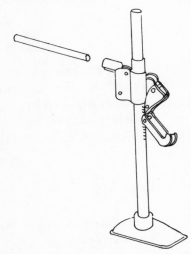

3. *The body jack.* Many foreign car manufacturers use this kind of jack. It has a fitting that goes into slots on either side of the car. It is inserted into one of the slots and is raised on the side that has the flat.

Instructions on how to use a jack are given in Chapter 4.

TIRE LUG WRENCH

This tool is used to remove the bolts on a wheel so that the wheel itself can be removed. I would advise you to ignore the one supplied by the auto manufacturer and buy one shaped like an X, as illustrated below.

Get a big one, since the more leverage you have, the less strength it takes to loosen the bolts. The lug wrenches supplied by car manufacturers are usually L-shaped and require the strength of an Atlas to budge the bolts.

WHEEL BLOCKS

These are items you can make yourself. Wheel blocks are used under the front wheel and/or under the rear wheel as a safety device to keep the car from rolling as you work

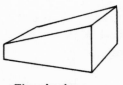

**Five inches
(approx.)**

on it. If you don't have wheel blocks, a log or rocks from the side of the road can be used. However, the wedge-shaped block is more efficient and fits easily into your trunk.

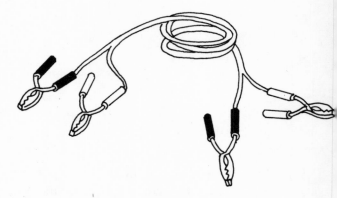

BATTERY "JUMPER" (BOOSTER) CABLES

This inexpensive item could be a lifesaver on a cold winter night when your battery decides to die. Electricity can be jumped from the battery of another car to your car battery, allowing your car to start. See Chapter 6 for details on how to use these cables.

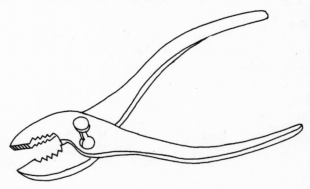

PLIERS, ADJUSTABLE (CRESCENT) WRENCH, SCREWDRIVER

As you can imagine, these tools are used for many and various problems that may come up: bolts to be turned, screws to be tightened, and so on.

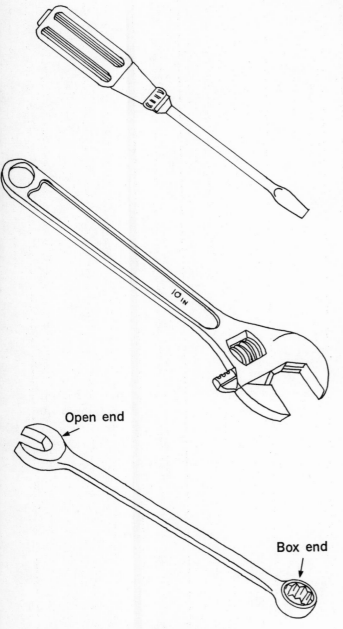

Open end

Box end

BOX AND OPEN-END WRENCH SET

A set of these wrenches is a worthwhile investment. Though you may never use them

yourself, if you are stranded by the side of the road, one of these wrenches and a knowledgeable helper could get you rolling again. If you drive a foreign car that is sized in meters, be sure to buy a set using this system in its measurements.

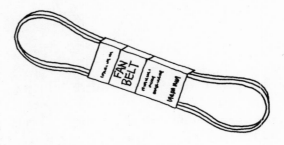

EXTRA FAN BELT

You will be in real trouble if the old fan belt breaks. You will be stuck! The belt drives the water pump and keeps the cooling water circulating with the fan. Or, if your car is air-cooled, like a Volkswagen, it keeps the fan turning, cooling oil and air. Without this cooling action, your car heats to a point where other functions are ruined.

Take a look at Chapter 7 for discussions on the cooling system.

FLASHLIGHT

For obvious reasons, this item is necessary. Get a good strong one with a powerful light

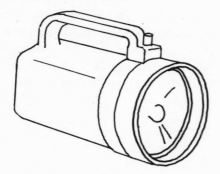

source. In fact, some come with a blinking red light on their back ends, which means the lamp can double as a warning light. (Even better for warning is a good supply of flares.)

FLARES

These lifesavers look like firecrackers and are fueled to give a bright hour's worth of light. They will burn even in the rain, snow, and wind, and will quickly inform other travelers that you are a motorist at the side of the road with a problem.

RAGS

Obviously, any kind of work around an auto is dirty work. You'll want a couple of rags tucked into a corner of the trunk and another soft rag more readily available to the driver for wiping fogged windows.

OLD RAINCOAT

This is not essential, but it is handy as a coverall when you must kneel on your slacks or stockings to change a tire in the mud.

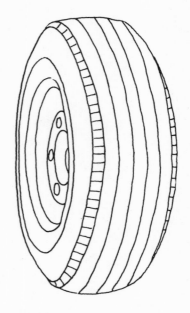

SPARE TIRE

This, of course, is a most important item. Be sure to have your spare checked frequently for proper pressure. It can go soft sitting in the trunk over a period of months. See Chapter 4 on how to change a tire.

EXTRA FUSES

Fuses protect all the electrical functions of your car, as they do those in your home. The fuse that blows might be the one that powers your headlights or windshield wipers. (This only seems to happen on dark rainy nights.)

So carry extras and know where the fuse panel is located. (Consult your auto manual.) The fuses clip on to their contact easily.

You might want to set up a labeling system for yourself.

For example:

Your own experience may suggest other tools to carry. It is impossible, however, to protect yourself against every event that may occur on the road. So use your judgment when selecting extra tools and consider seriously the recommendations in this chapter.

2. THE BODY BEAUTIFUL

It's HARD TO believe that anyone would spend $4,000 for a beautiful, shiny automobile and in less than a year let it become a dirty, dull, decrepit-looking mass of metal. But there are people who do.

I am confident that since you are reading this book, you take some pride in your auto and want its body to look as good and stay as sound as the day it was delivered.

Let's start right in with the cleaning and maintenance of your proud chariot.

Keeping Your Car Clean and Polished

CLEANSING AND PAMPERING THE BODY

Get yourself a bucket, sprinkle in a handful of mild soap powder, and fill the bucket with cool water. Don't use a strong floor-scrubbing soap. In fact, the soap you use for your undies is not too delicate for your car. Treat the satin finish of your auto gently. Don't use any scrubbing brushes or abrasive materials when washing the body. *Never* use steel wool on stubborn spots. A big, soft sponge is best.

Work from top to bottom. Rinse off all the soap, and wipe the car dry with a soft shammy (chamois) to avoid water stains. A shammy is a soft suede cloth. It should be thoroughly wet, wrung out, and then laid flat on the car. Slowly pull the shammy along the length of a fender and see how surprisingly dry the fender is left. Dry the entire car this way. Work in the shade for proper results—the sun will burn in water and soap spots.

WASHING THE WHEELS

A stronger soap can be used here, since tires and wheels generally take the worst of the road dirt. Go right at them with elbow grease and a scrubbing brush, especially if you have whitewalls. You can purchase a whitewall cleaner if you choose.

If you live in a cold climate, one of your big enemies will be salted or chemically treated icy roads. These are a major cause of body corrosion and rust. If your car is subjected to these conditions throughout the winter, it might be wise to inquire about having the body rustproofed, although this is rather costly. The rustproofing uses a sealant that is sprayed on the underbody and inside the body panels. The sealant creeps into the smallest nooks and crannies. If you decide on this treatment, be sure that a good, long guarantee is given with the job. A poorly done job will only trap the water and encourage rust.

If you forgo rustproofing, make frequent trips to an auto laundry. Be sure the force spray gets underneath your car and washes away the damaging salt that may have accumulated inside fenders and beneath doors.

WAXING AND POLISHING

Waxing a car may seem like a lot of work, but it's not done just for beauty's sake. One of the best forms of protection you can give a car against rain, snow, sun, and dirt is a good wax polish. To prove a point, just notice how water stays on the surface of an unwaxed car. Then note how the water rolls off that same surface after waxing. Also, dirt and dust are abrasive to a shiny metal surface. But if that surface has a protective coating of wax on it, only the wax will be damaged on a dusty road.

So whether you pay to have it done or do it yourself, *make sure it's done!*

HOW TO WAX

Twice a year is a must for giving your car a good waxing, once in the spring and once in the fall (when a good, thorough one is needed in anticipation of winter).

Waxing a car is very difficult to do on a cold day, and just as difficult on a hot, humid day. Under a hot sun, you will just smear the wax around. A temperature between 60° and 75° on a clear, dry day is ideal.

Gather together three soft cotton rags (not nylon, wool, or rayon—these tend to smear the wax). One rag is for wax application, the second for rubbing, and the third for buffing.

Of course, the best kind of wax is the hardest to use. This is the old-fashioned paste kind that comes in the short, squat can. Lots of elbow grease is needed, but the job will last you nicely for six months.

The well-known liquid brands that come in bottles or tall cans are effective—but you'd better plan on doing the job more often. Waxing, however, will be easier and quicker.

Follow the directions given with the product, and work about two square feet at a time, rubbing the wax on in a circular motion. Then rub off with a clean cloth and buff with another clean cloth.

Concentrate on the under panels, working section by section. These areas take a lot of weathering and muddy splashing, so be liberal with wax. In fact, doing these areas twice to build up a wax protection is worthwhile.

Put effort into the roof, engine hood, and trunk lid. These surfaces take the battering rain and the beating, color-fading sun.

Wax all metal surfaces: bumpers, hubcaps, door handles, and even the radio antenna. These chrome and aluminum surfaces will be less susceptible to that ugly pitting you've seen.

AVOIDING OR CONTENDING WITH DIRT

Now, after you've put a lot of effort into a polish, if you're lucky enough to have a garage, use it! There are too many garages overflowing with $50 bicycles, $3 basketballs, $10 ladders, and worthless newspapers while the $3,000 car stands in the driveway in the sleet, rain, and snow. The garage will do more to prolong the life of your car than anything else.

We've talked about winter salt and weather, but springtime can also bring all kinds of unexpected dirt sources. Trees drip tiny droplets of gooey sap, well-fed birds sit in those same trees, and on a mild night a profusion of insects will be attracted to your headlights: splato! You can't avoid these things, but it's wise to clean up after them.

Parking on the street in the middle of a stickball game could cause all kinds of problems. Give the kids and your car a break, and park around the corner.

Parking near a construction site can make quite a dusty mess of your car. If you see one of these sites, park a couple of blocks away.

Trouble-Free Windows and Doors

WINDOWS

Windows that sparkle are nice, but niceness isn't the main reason for cleanliness. Safety is! Obviously, the clearer you can see, the safer you can drive.

Instructions on how to clean windows may seem unnecessary—just some water and a rag, and look how they sparkle in the sunlight! But get out on a busy roadway at night and suddenly every street light and headlight becomes an elongated glaring smear on your windshield. Water is not enough to cut through road film and grease accumulations. It *will* get rid of dirt, but it leaves the "stubborns" smeared all over the glass.

Use a mild, grease-cutting detergent, a soft rag, and some vigor to clean the glass thoroughly. Be careful of the glass-cleaning prod-

ucts on the market. Some may suds up if mixed with the film left behind by the liquid in your car's window washer and could cause an awful mess when next you use the washer and wipers. Try different glass-cleaning products and see which one satisfies you.

Don't neglect the back and side windows. And, of course, the inside can get just as dirty as the outside, especially if smokers ride in your car. It's astonishing to see the amount of residue that comes off on your rag after an hour or two of heavy smoking.

Windshield wipers. Make sure your windshield wipers are in good shape, and that the rubber blades are fresh and clean. New blades are not costly, and most gas stations keep them in stock. The attendant can snap them on in minutes. Be aware that if the rubber blades are dry or worn down so that the metal fittings rub on the glass, the window can be badly scratched.

Automatic windshield washer. This is a most valuable mechanism that now comes installed in all autos sold in the United States.

I'm sure you've driven in a drizzle and have had a car pass you in another lane and spray you liberally with mucky, gritty water. A flick of a button and your washer has cleared the windshield nicely. So be sure the washer container is filled with water and a washer solution. This solution prevents the liquid from freezing in the winter and contains a detergent that helps clean the windshield more effectively.

Consult your auto manual for the location of this water container.

Winter treatment. In icy, snowy weather, be sure to keep a plastic windshield scraper to help you clean away ice. Metal- or glass-edged scrapers will leave permanent scratches.

DOORS

DON'T SLAM THE DOOR! A most repeated refrain, especially around children. This command refers to auto doors as well as the porch screen door. Just compare the two and you'll see which has the more complicated mechanism and which can be damaged more easily with constant slamming.

If hinges and latches are well lubricated and aligned with one another, there's no need to shut the door violently to secure a proper latch. Here are some of the things that can happen from constant slamming:

1. Window glass can break.
2. Latch and lock mechanisms can jar and either rattle badly or not work at all.
3. The "striker" mechanism, which holds the door in a closed position, can loosen, allowing the door to fly open.
4. Window cranks can loosen, so that windows raise and lower with difficulty.

I won't go any further; I think you get my point.

Sometimes it helps to open the window an inch. This reduces the pressure within the car, making the door close more easily.

Lubrication. Door hinges and latches and trunk and hood latches should be given a squirt of light oil periodically.

Locks should be given a shot of lock-cylinder lubricant, especially before winter sets in. Have you ever been trapped outside your car in a blizzard because the lock is frozen and your key won't work? Just thinking about it should hurry you to the hardware store.

Be careful if there's a freeze after a rainstorm. Weatherstripping around a door or trunk lid can become frozen and be stripped away by a sharp yank. Coat the weatherstripping with a spray preparation sold at auto supply stores.

Vinyl Roofs

A major part of maintenance is cleanliness. Use a mild, grease-cutting detergent on your vinyl roof. A soft-bristle brush can be used to scrub out the grime. A special vinyl top cleaner is also available. A vinyl top dressing may also be bought. As your car gets older, this dressing will help preserve and waterproof the roof.

Convertible Tops

If you are a convertible enthusiast, you have an additional set of maintenance difficulties with which to contend. However, if you are a *true* enthusiast, you won't consider these things "difficulties."

THE TOP FOLDING MECHANISM

If you pilot a little sports car with a manual top, there are fewer things that can go wrong than if you drive a car with a power-operated top. To operate the manual top, you usually loosen a top fastener of some sort and lower the top by hand, making sure none of the fabric pinches in the folding mechanism. Occasionally give the folding joints of the top's frame a squirt of machine oil. Be careful not to get oil on the fabric of the top or on the plastic window.

Most convertible tops are automatic and work on a hydraulic-electric system. If, at the touch of a button, nothing happens, check the fuse. If this is not at fault, it will probably mean a trip to your dealer.

However, having an automatic top does not eliminate the necessity of lubricating the joints and taking care that the top doesn't pinch in these joints.

CONVERTIBLE BACK WINDOWS

Before unzipping the back window, it's a good idea to lower the top slightly. This loosens the whole top, making unzipping easier. Lubricate the zipper occasionally, using a clear lubricant. Vaseline jelly, or even better, a Vaseline stick, works very well.

The plastic window must be treated with tender loving care because it scratches very easily. Never use an ice scraper on this window. Never use hot water on it, and never clean it with a dry rag. Use a solution of mild soap and tepid or cool water, and wash the plastic window with a sponge. Dry it with a soft cloth. No strong detergents or solvents such as turpentine or alcohol should be used. Remember that in freezing weather the plastic window becomes very brittle, and if you should decide to lower the top, you could crack this window. Many recent-model convertibles have glass rear windows.

Here are some "never nevers" for convertible owners:

1. Never lower or raise the top while the car is in motion. Even when moving slowly, the pressure of air is quite strong and could rip the top and its mechanism out by the roots.
2. Never lower the top in freezing weather. Driving along bundled up on a bright cold day with cheeks aglow is invigorating, but common sense should tell you that the top will be brittle and the mechanism stiff. You could cause damage.
3. Never lower the top into a top well that has items stored in it. It's a good way to punch a hole in the top.

FABRIC MAINTENANCE

Clean your top with a mild, grease-cutting detergent, tepid or cool water, and a soft-bristled brush. Always clean with the grain of the fabric. The same top cleaner mentioned in the section on vinyl roofs can be used here. Rinse well.

Top dressing is available for the top as it grows older. This dressing keeps the fabric supple, helps waterproof the top, and helps mantain the color. Some dressings are painted on, some are sponged, and some sprayed. Read the directions in the store, and buy the one that suits you best.

Refinishing the Body

A NEW PAINT JOB

The paints used by U.S. manufacturers today are synthetic acrylic lacquers or enamels. These are sprayed on at the factory and then baked at extremely high temperatures for quick drying. The baking procedure is completed before the installation of the glass and rubber components of the car, as they cannot tolerate the extreme temperatures. These acrylics dry to a sparkle, with no factory polishing necessary.

If you plan to have your car repainted, it is best to seek out a shop that will use acrylic lacquer. This procedure omits the baking step, but the paint takes longer to dry. Because of the slow drying, some polish rubbing is necessary. The finish will be much more durable than the standard enamel used by many shops. As you might imagine, the acrylic lacquer job is more expensive.

If you plan to have just a portion of your car repainted, you are taking a gamble on the color match. An older car may have a finish that is somewhat faded. Most shops will make no guarantee as to match. However, in a year or so the newly painted portion will probably have "weathered in."

Don't consider painting the car yourself. It's time-consuming, you must have a proper place to work, and you must have a good knowledge of what you're doing. If you're determined to attempt it, there are books available on the subject.

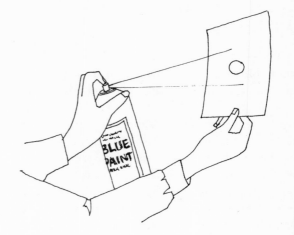

TOUCH-UPS

With care and patience you can do quite an effective job of touching up nicks, scratches, and stains.

Most auto supply stores sell spray cans of touch-up paint. These paints are often labeled "1969 Plymouth green" or "1971 Ford light blue." Or perhaps there will be an identifying color chart at the paint counter.

To prevent future rusting, you will need a spray can of body primer or rustproofing. You'll also need medium-grit, fine-grit, and superfine-grit emery paper and a can of rubbing compound.

1. *Sanding.* Clean away dirt and loose rust. Working in one direction, sand the offending area with medium-grit paper. Sand until all signs of rust or stain are gone and shiny raw metal shows through. If you're working on a dime-sized chip, sand until the edges are smooth and they blend into the painted car. The working area will now probably be the size of a silver dollar.

2. *Priming.* Work in an area where there's no breeze and as little dust as possible to be trapped in this wet paint. Wipe away your sanding dust and, using tape and old newspapers, mask off any door handles, headlights, or chrome bumpers you don't want painted.

   If you're doing a dollar-sized area, cut a hole in a piece of cardboard, hold the cardboard about three inches away from the car, and spray with the primer or rustproofer.

Of course, if you're spraying a larger area, the cardboard with the hole cannot be used.

Spray the area smoothly, keeping the button on the can depressed steadily to avoid start-and-stop spatters and spits. Apply a thin layer of primer, let it dry, apply another thin layer. Do this three times, and the area should be well covered.

3. *Sanding the primer.* Using superfine emery paper, gently sand the primed area while a helper dribbles water onto the area with a garden hose. This is called wet sanding and will give you a superfine satinlike finish. Don't sand so vigorously that you sand away all your primer. Sand in one direction only.

4. *Spraying the proper color.* Shake the can of proper color thoroughly. Again, for that small, dollar-sized spot, use the cardboard with the hole exactly the way you did with the primer. A larger area would be handled like the prime coat, without the cardboard. Spray on each coat very thinly, let it dry, and spray again. Do this five or six times, waiting ten minutes for drying each time.

5. *The final rubbing.* Let the built-up coats of color dry at least twenty-four

hours. Then apply a rubbing compound product to a soft rag and lightly rub in a circular motion around the edges until they blend into the original finish. Then work in the area until you have a high luster. Rub evenly and do not concentrate on one spot, as you can rub right through your new paint to bare metal again.

6. *Wax.* A week or so later, using a paste wax, protect the newly finished area.

FIBERGLASS PATCHING

Fiberglass patching kits are available in your auto supply store. These kits can be used for patching fist-sized rusted-out areas on your car. They contain a few pieces of fiberglass (this looks like woven cloth), resin, and hardener.

1. Chip out and wire-brush away as much rust as possible. Sandpaper away as much more rust as possible.
2. Follow the directions enclosed in the fiberglass kit carefully, and apply the resin, fiberglass, and hardener.
3. When completely dry, sand the whole area smooth. Then paint the area as explained earlier.

Everything I have explained in this chapter is a money-saving task that you can do yourself.

····3. HOUSEKEEPING

YOUR CAR, LIKE your home, gets cluttered and dusty and must be swept just as diligently.

Candy wrappers, umbrellas, newspapers, and leaves can accumulate at an alarming rate, and grime from shoes deposits itself liberally over the floor mats.

A worthwhile investment is a plug-in electric hand vacuum. I say "plug-in" because the battery-operated ones, though convenient, are usually not as efficient.

Hand vacuums generally have attachments for upholstery, the cracks and crevices between and under seats, and, of course, floor carpets. Usually the floorboards of a car are lower than the floor sill and are very difficult to broom-sweep. The vacuum works nicely.

Upholstery

Following are some hints on how to clean your upholstery, whether vinyl, cloth, or leather.

VINYL UPHOLSTERY

Special cleaners may be purchased for your vinyl upholstery, but for general grime cleaning with a sponge, rustle up some detergent suds in a bucket of warm water. Scoop up only the suds on the sponge and rub lightly, repeatedly scooping up more suds. With a damp cloth, wipe up all detergent. Dry the

17

vinyl with a fresh cloth. Don't soak the upholstery, as moisture could get into and damage the upholstery padding.

CLOTH UPHOLSTERY

Your cloth upholstery is more difficult to clean. Most stains are removable with a volatile cleaning fluid like carbon tetrachloride. Work in a well-ventilated place with car windows open. Do not douse the area with carbon tet, and don't rub it in vigorously. Gently apply the cleaner, and blot the area dry with absorbent paper toweling.

Little children and puppies (and sometimes you and I) can raise all sorts of havoc in autos. Here are hints for specific cleanups. (All these spots should be cleaned as quickly as possible.)

Candy. Rub with a sponge dampened with warm water and detergent suds. Chocolate candy gets special treatment: wipe the spot with a sponge soaked in tepid soap suds and, while the candy is wet, scrape it with the dull edge of a knife.

Grass. Rub with a sponge dampened with warm water and detergent suds.

Shoe polish. Scrape off the excess. Rub gently with cleaning fluid, turning the cloth often.

Vomit. Clean up with rags. Sponge spot with cold water. Then wash the area gently with mild soap and lukewarm water. Rub again with a mixture of six parts cold water to one part clear household ammonia.

Urine. Sponge stains with lukewarm water and mild suds. Then sponge-rinse. Wet a clean rag with a mixture of one part clear household ammonia to six parts cool water.

Place the rag over the area for about a minute, and then rub with a clean damp cloth.

Battery acid. Saturate the area with clear household ammonia to neutralize the acid. Then rinse with cold water.

Grease or oil. Remove as much of it as possible with the dull edge of a knife. Then rub the area with cleaning fluid, turning the cloth often.

Tar. Scrape off as much as possible with the dull edge of a knife. Then use cleaning fluid, turning the rag often.

LEATHER UPHOLSTERY

Leather upholstery is handsome but very vulnerable and must be cleaned gently. Avoid using saddle soap, as it is a grime collector. Rub a cake of mild soap on a damp soft absorbent cloth until a light whipped-creamlike lather appears. Rub this onto the leather, cleaning a small area at a time. Wipe the lather off with a clean damp rag. Then polish with a clean dry cloth. Specific cleaners can be purchased for leather if you prefer to use them.

Floors

It's a good idea to buy a set of floor mats for the much-used front floor area of your car.

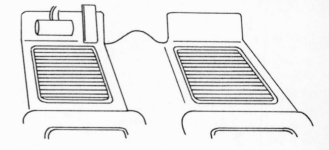

These are usually made of rubber and fit in the flat area beneath your feet.

Mats serve two purposes. First, they help protect the actual floor from wear, and second, they make for easy removal of dirt. Lift out each floor mat and shake it. When they're really dirty, take them out, scrub them with detergent, and hose them down.

Stowage Space

Many mysterious rattles turn out to be unfastened spare tires or loose flashlights. Try to have a specific place for everything that is kept in the car. Be sure the spare tire is secured in its nest just as the manufacturer planned. Tools should be kept in a tool box, but if that box is metal you can have a lot of clanking around in the box. Since you should carry rags, try wrapping the tools in the rags for quiet.

Here is a list of handy items to have in the trunk and glove compartment of your car, in addition to the items mentioned in Chapter 1.

1. Fire extinguisher (there are very compact and inexpensive models available)
2. Maps
3. First-aid kit and first-aid book
4. Pencil and paper

The glove compartment is small enough, so avoid filling it with unnecessary items like gloves.

Keep the rear shelf clear. You won't be able to use your rear-view mirror effectively if you can't see out the rear window.

Empty ashtrays to avoid cigarette fires.

Keep the windows clean, as discussed in Chapter 2.

Now that your car is clean inside and out, let's go on to some technical information.

4. TIRES

As YOU MIGHT suspect, a tire is not just a hollow rubber tube full of air. In fact, a tire is a very sophisticated combination of fibers, steel, fabric, and rubber, which has taken many years of research to develop.

TIRE CONSTRUCTION

Let's talk about a dull subject: tire construction. You will need to know certain terminology when you go to purchase tires.

Bias-ply tires. These tires come either two-bias-ply or four-bias-ply (or to confuse the matter more, two-bias-ply rated at four). Pictured below is the four-bias-ply tire, illustrating the four layers of material crisscrossed onto the tire. If you sawed the tire in half it would look like this.

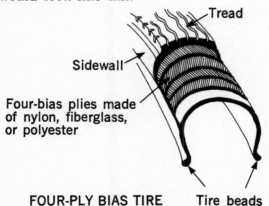

FOUR-PLY BIAS TIRE

Belted-bias-ply tires. This is one of the better tires available today. It's a good basic tire, although it is more expensive than the four-bias-ply tire. The combination of plies laid in opposing directions and belts laid over the circumference of the plies give the tire its great strength, durability, and road-firmness. For the additional cost of this tire, you can expect double the service and mileage.

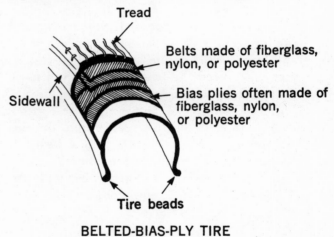

BELTED-BIAS-PLY TIRE

Radial tires. Possibly the best tire available to date is the radial tire. At high speeds the ride is comfortable, and at low speeds the car has a firm, confident feel on the road. It is reputed to be durable and safe. The tread of the tire stays flush with the road when you turn the wheel—there is no squeeze or pinch on the tread when turning. You will have great protection against punctures and impact damage. This tire is so efficient you may even notice an increase in your gas mileage. Radial tires cannot be mixed with other types of tires. You must have all four radial tires on the car to be assured of proper handling.

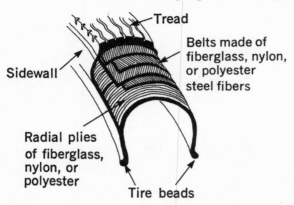

RADIAL TIRE
Two-radial plies with four belts

Your choice of tire should, of course, depend upon the type of driving you do. Consult with your tire dealer for a complete evaluation of your needs. If you baby your car, drive once a week to the grocery store and once a year to the mountains, naturally you won't need the best, toughest, and most durable tires available, and don't let anyone talk you into them. However, if you grind back and forth at the speed limit on the throughway every day in all kinds of weather, the best tire is worth the investment.

If you buy a new car, check what type tire comes as standard equipment. You may choose to buy a better one.

TIRE SIZES

Nowadays most of the tire industry uses the same coding system to designate the size of any tire.

For instance: H78–15. The letter H desig-

nates the tire's load-carrying capacity. The higher the letter, the greater the capacity. For example, a Pinto has a load-carrying capacity of A, which is sufficient for this little car. Compare it to the capacity of a Chevrolet Impala, whch is rated at G, and you will know why it is not recommended that you carry a cast-iron antique stove in your Pinto.

Before a federal law was passed requiring the manufacturer to state the load capacity, consumers were badly abused by the vagueness of the manufacturer's specifications.

The number 78 refers to the percentage ratio of the tire's height to its width. In other words, this tire is 78% as high as it is wide.

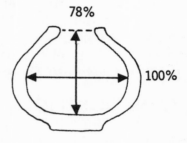

The number 15 means that this tire fits onto a fifteen-inch wheel.

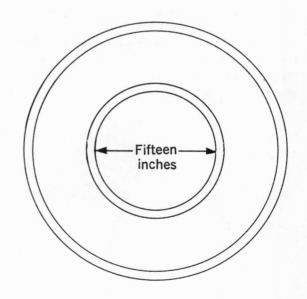

Another example is HR78–15.*

H = Load capacity.
R = Radial ply tire.
78 = Percentage ratio of tire height to width.
15 = Fifteen-inch rim size.

TUBELESS TIRES

Most· of today's tires are tubeless; inner tubes are used only occasionally. Today it is rare for a modern tire to go instantly flat, causing loss of control and potential accident.

Many clean punctures (as from a nail) can be mended temporarily—but only temporarily —by having a plug inserted into the hole at a garage. I would advise replacing the tire or having it mended at a garage, with a vulcanized plug and a vulcanized patch.

A slow leak can often be remedied by putting an inner tube inside the tubeless tire.

A damaged sidewall usually means replacing the tire.

SNOW TIRES

Snow tires for your car are close to a must if you live in an area where snow and sleet are factors. Driving with conventional tires in a snowstorm can produce a very dangerous situation.

However, when the snow season has passed, it is definitely advisable to go back to conventional tires. They are quieter and easier to drive on. Also, snow tires can be damaged in hot weather by the heat friction that is

* Occasionally a manufacturer will use the metric measure to indicate the tire's height and width. For instance, 185 X 70 X 15: 185 refers to the tire's height and 70 to its width in millimeters; the 15 refers to the rim size of the actual wheel and is given in inches. Why these two measuring systems are mixed is a question no one seems able to answer. In this marking system there is no coding for the load capacity.

generated when driving at high speeds on a sizzling parkway.

Snow tires with studs. Even on the slickest ice, these tires will give you traction. Steel studs embedded in the tires and protruding 1/32 to 1/16 inch beyond the tire's surface are amazingly effective. However, these same studs can cause damage to the road's surface and therefore are prohibited in some areas and on some roads. Check regulations in your area before buying studded snow tires.

THE LIFE OF THE TIRE

The way you drive. One of the most effective ways to prolong the life of your tire is by common sense and good driving. In other words:

No screech-away starts.
No neck-jarring stops (unless necessary for safety).
Slow down when rounding a corner.
Drive slowly and with care in a road construction area.
Keep your eye out for winter potholes or frost-lifted pavement.
When parking, don't bump or rub the curb.

Tire pressure. Keeping your tires at the manufacturer's recommended pressure is very important to the life of your tire. The correct pressure is stamped right on the side of the tire. For additional recommendations on pressure, check your auto manual. The manual will often recommend a difference in the pressure of the back and front tires. Observe this. If there is a big difference (five pounds or more) between the tire manufacturer's recommendation and the auto manual, write the tire manufacturer, telling him the year and model of your car, and ask him why this discrepancy exists.

Too much pressure (overinflation) causes the center of the tread to bulge outward and thus to wear faster than the edges. The car will ride very hard, and every little bump will be felt by you as well as your car's suspension system. The tire will also be very vulnerable to obstacles on bad roads.

Worn

Because driving at high speeds in hot weather can build up pressure in your tires, it is wise to keep your tires *slightly* underinflated.

Low pressure results in bad handling and heat build-up, which can very quickly ruin a tire.

Worn

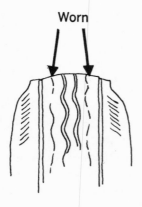

Normal inward or outward tilt of the wheels is called camber (see Chapter 11). Too much camber can wear the tire on its inner or outer edge. Have your wheel balance and alignment checked periodically. A good time to do this is when the tires are rotated.

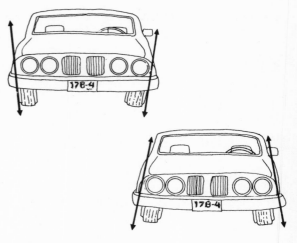

Tire Rotation. Change your tires around about every 5,000 miles. This distributes the wear of the tires more evenly. A recommended rotation is shown here:

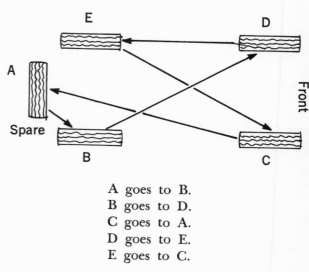

A goes to B.
B goes to D.
C goes to A.
D goes to E.
E goes to C.

Make sure your garage man checks the alignment and balance of the wheels at this time. If the alignment and balance are out of adjustment, they can cause wear. The mechanic will often position lead weights on the wheel rim to help the balance.

Additional hints. Remove any embedded bits of glass or pebbles from the tire with narrow-nosed pliers.

Be careful not to overload the car. If the tires were designed to hold six adults and their normal baggage, and you add a roof rack with camping gear, you will probably add strain to your tires and suspension.

A quick way to check the wear of the tread on your tire is to take a dime and insert it top side down into the groove of the tread. If the top of Mr. Roosevelt's head shows, your tread is worn enough to seriously consider new tires.

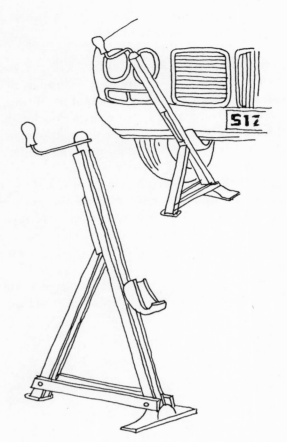

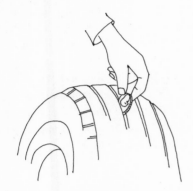

CHANGING A TIRE

Here are two of the jacks available to you.

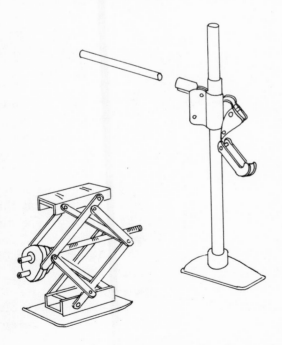

and stable, and cranking up the car requires little effort.

Here are two of the lug wrenches available for removing the tire.

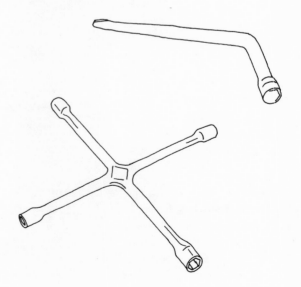

I recommend the crank-handled bumper jack as the one easier to use. Its base is broad

As I mentioned in Chapter 1, I heartily recommend the X-shaped one.

Step-by-step tire changes. Flat tires are the result of a variety of mishaps. A sudden flat can be caused by picking up a nail or running over something that cuts or tears. No longer does the driver have to fear sudden blowouts; they are very rare with the improved modern tire. A sudden flat usually deflates gradually enough that you become aware of it before it causes a mishap. Some other flat-makers are stones that bruise, defective rims that separate from the rubber, weakened rubber valve stems, or valve cores that are corroded and leaky.

But regardless of what causes the flat, the fact remains that now you're stuck at the side of an empty road. OK. Down on your knees and change it! It's easy, and I'll explain it step by step.

1. If you're facing an upgrade, position wedges, blocks of wood, or, if it's the only thing available, a rock, in back of the downhill side of both the front and rear wheels.

    If facing a downgrade, place the wedges under your front and rear wheels on the downhill side. Turn the front wheels into the curb.

    If you're undecided which way the earth is tilting, put blocks all over the place to be sure. These blocks, as you may have figured out, keep the car from rolling as you work.

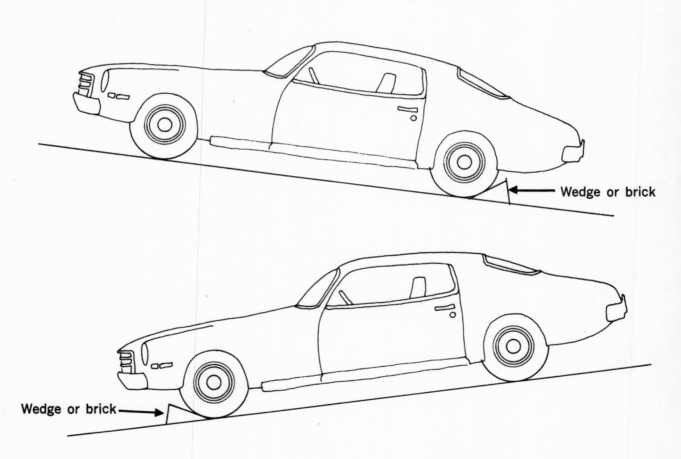

Wedge or brick

Wedge or brick

2. Insert a screwdriver between the hub-cap and the wheel at various places around the cap and pry the hubcap off. (The car should not be jacked up yet.)

3. Take the lug wrench and *loosen slightly but do not remove* the five (occasionally four or six) big nuts that were hidden by the hubcap. The reason you loosen these before jacking up is that the nuts are difficult to loosen with the wheel off the ground, since the wheel will then turn freely as you try to turn the nut.

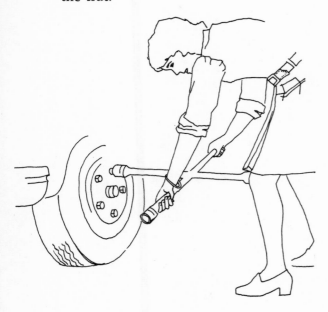

4. Now jack up the car. Assuming you have the standard Detroit-supplied bumper jack, set the base of it under the bumper and raise the lip until it hooks under the bumper on the side of the affected tire. There should be instructions on how to use this jack in your auto manual.

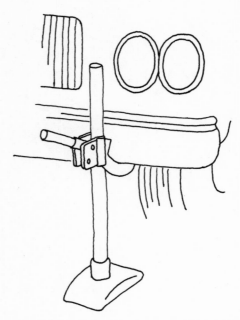

Continue to raise the jack until the jack has lifted the tire two or three inches off the ground.

5. Remove the loosened lug nuts, taking them off in the sequence illustrated below. This lessens the strain on the wheel as you remove it.

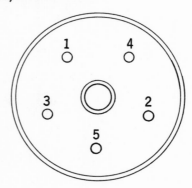

6. Now that all the nuts are off, place them in the bowl-shaped hubcap so they don't get lost. Pull the wheel off. It's heavy, so be careful. Put the spare tire on, lining up the holes in the spare with the bolts sticking out of the wheel.

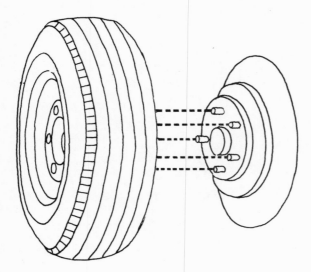

7. Hand-screw the big nuts on again in the same sequence used removing them. You will notice that these nuts are slightly conical in shape. Be sure to screw them on with the flat side facing you. The conical taper helps center the wheel onto the hub. While the car is jacked up, tighten the nuts as tight as you can with the lug wrench. Be sure the tire is now on straight and flush against the wheel hub.

8. Lower the car by lowering the jack until the tire is on the ground. Remove the jack.

9. Tighten the lug bolts as tight as you can now that the car is back on the ground. Replace the hubcap and remove the wedges.

Changing a tire is not difficult. Just follow each step closely and don't get upset. You'll be on your way in a surprisingly short time.

5. THE GASOLINE SYSTEM

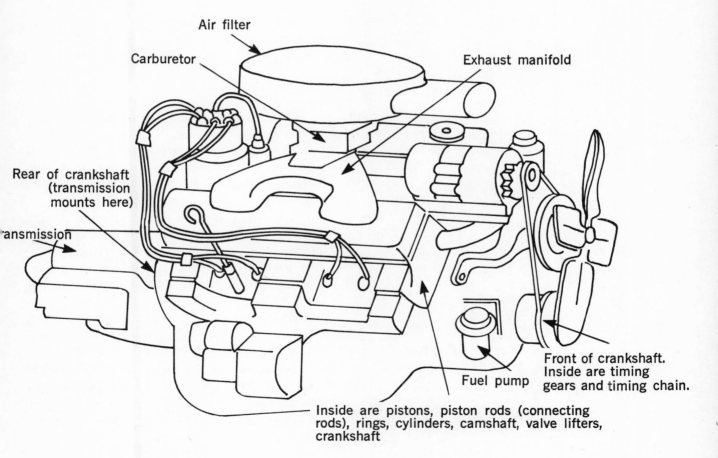

Air filter

Carburetor

Exhaust manifold

Rear of crankshaft
(transmission
mounts here)

Transmission

Front of crankshaft.
Inside are timing
gears and timing chain.

Fuel pump

Inside are pistons, piston rods (connecting
rods), rings, cylinders, camshaft, valve lifters,
crankshaft

Listed here are some major parts directly involved in your auto's fuel system:

Fuel pump   Carburetor
Fuel tank   Intake manifold
Fuel line   Combustion chambers
Fuel filter

The following items are related to your fuel system:

Pistons   Exhaust manifold
Cylinders   Muffler and exhaust pipes
Crankshaft   Tailpipe
Air cleaner

In the illustration below you can follow the path gasoline takes when you turn on the engine.

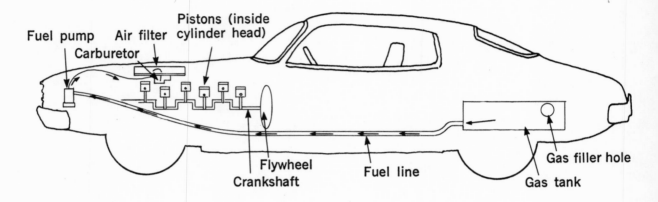

FUEL PUMP

The fuel pump draws gasoline from the gas tank and pumps it through the fuel line. It then pumps gasoline up and into the carburetor.

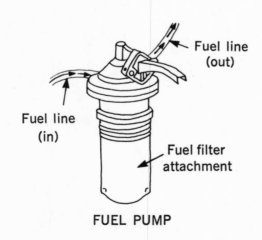

FUEL PUMP

CARBURETOR

Gasoline must be proportionately mixed with air in order to start and run the engine. This mixing is the carburetor's job. Attached above the carburetor is a large filter that cleans the air before it is drawn into the carburetor.

The fuel pump, at the same time, pumps gasoline into the carburetor's float chamber. (Some cars use a fuel injection mechanism for each cylinder that replaces the float chamber system.) With the float chamber is the gas jet. Fuel is drawn into this barrel-shaped attachment along with air. Then this fuel-air vaporizes and the combination passes into the intake manifold.

When you are waiting for a light to change your engine is idling. There are mechanisms in the carburetor that adjust to supply just enough fuel-air to keep the engine running.

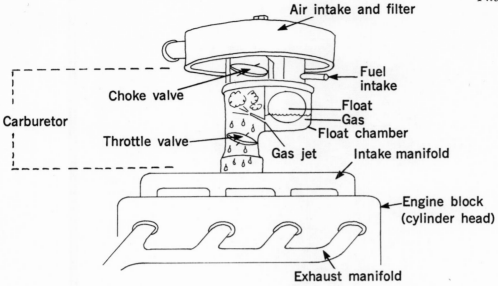

When you press the accelerator pedal to move, or to go faster, more fuel-air is necessary. When your car is under stress, climbing a steep hill, or pulling a heavy load, parts of the carburetor adjust for a proper fuel-air combination. As you can see, the carburetor is a very important and delicate portion of your engine and needs regular care and adjustment by your mechanic.

On to the next step.

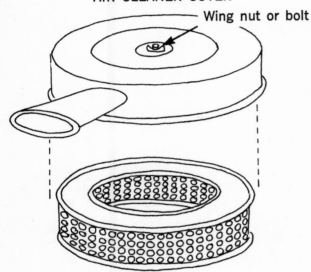

INTAKE MANIFOLD

The intake manifold guides the fuel-air into each combustion chamber.

COMBUSTION CHAMBERS (CYLINDERS)

Depending on whether you have a four-, six-, or eight-cylinder car, you will have four, six, or eight combustion chambers, pistons, and spark plugs. When you turn on the ignition to start the engine, the proper amount of fuel-air is released into each combustion chamber, coming first from the carburetor and then from the intake manifold. The starter motor (see Chapter 6) forces the pistons in the chamber to move upward and downward, compressing the fuel-air in the chamber with every other upward stroke. The compressed fuel-air in each combustion chamber is ignited, one by one in sequence, by each spark plug. As the spark plug ignites the fuel-air mixture, a miniature explosion occurs within the combustion chamber, forcing the piston, now in its up position, to go down. In other words, these continuing "explosions" in your motor as it runs cause the pistons to continue their up-and-down motions, and the

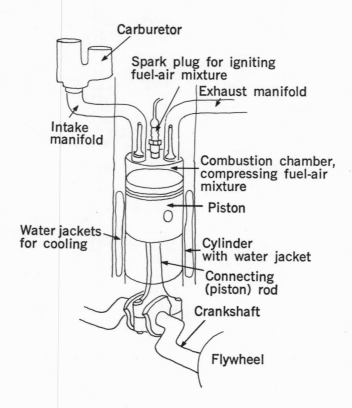

Carburetor

Spark plug for igniting
fuel-air mixture

Exhaust manifold

Intake
manifold

Combustion chamber,
compressing fuel-air
mixture

Piston

Water jackets
for cooling

Cylinder
with water jacket

Connecting
(piston) rod

Crankshaft

Flywheel

These are the four movements made by each
piston to complete one (four-stroke) cycle of
compression:

Fuel-air
mixture
being
drawn into
cylinder

Fuel-air mixture
being compressed upward

Spark plug has ignited
mixture, causing miniature
explosion, forcing
piston downward

Exhaust or waste from
explosion is forced
through the exhaust
manifold, and eventually
out through tailpipe

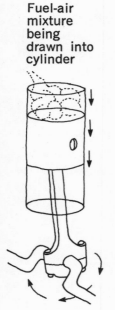

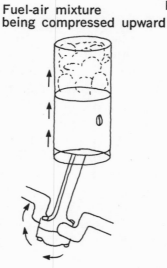

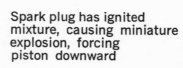

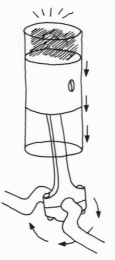

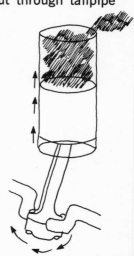

FUEL INTAKE STROKE   COMPRESSION STROKE   POWER STROKE   EXHAUST STROKE

up-and-down motions continue the explosions of the motor, thus completing and renewing each cycle.

Each of the four, six, or eight pistons is attached to a cranklike bar called a crankshaft. As the pistons go up and down, the crankshaft is rotated, making the flywheel at the crankshaft's end spin. The flywheel is attached by way of the crankshaft to a series of gears called the transmission. The transmission in turn regulates the spinning motion for power for the wheels.

This whole explanation has been simplified; I mention only the major components that come into action. There are other complex parts involved in completing these actions, but I think the preceding explanation will help you understand the essentials without going into more technical detail.

CHOKE

Most automobiles today have automatic chokes. The choke allows a richer (more gasoline than usual) fuel-air mixture to reach the carburetor for starting.

An often-used and manufacturer-recommended formula for starting, especially in cold weather, is:

1. Pump the gas pedal once. This automatically allows the richer mixture into the carburetor.
2. Wait four or five seconds to allow the fuel-air mixture to form properly.
3. Turn on the ignition. The car should start nicely.

However, a car can be as individual as a person. Variations for starting are sometimes necessary to find the key to your car's disposition. For instance, I had a little jewel that ran beautifully for eleven years and was still untarnished when I sold it. But it wouldn't start unless I pumped the gas pedal four times

and counted to twenty slowly—one thousand one, one thousand two, one thousand three, one thousand four. . . . This routine was the key, and the car and I got along famously as long as I didn't become impatient on this one point. It took two months to discover the formula, so have patience with your new car if it seems to be temperamental.

GRADES OF GASOLINE

This is a subject that has become more complicated for the average driver in recent years. When you pull into a modern service station, you often have the choice of *low test, regular, high test, high test with low lead, super high test, unleaded gas,* and even *diesel*. Which should you buy? The manual that came with your car may not explain this.

Lead-free or low-lead gasolines. These gasolines were developed to help combat air pollution. The exhaust from engines using leaded fuel contains harmful matter, but this matter is reduced or eliminated from the exhaust of cars using lead-free or low-lead gasoline. These gasolines also allow manufacturers to use catalytic mufflers, which oxidize the exhaust and reduce its carbon monoxide content.

Lead-free gas was developed for use in American cars from 1971 models through the present. It can also be used in a few earlier models. Check with your dealer or mechanic to find out if your car can use lead-free gas. Some autos will not be able to use this lead-free fuel because they require a higher octane gasoline. (Octane measures the antiknock properties of gasoline.) Lead-free or low-lead gas cannot be used in high-compression ratio engines; it can severely damage the valves. So ask the dealer about your make and model. If your car won't accept this fuel, don't use it or you'll have all sorts of annoyances. Your engine could knock, run unevenly, or just act cranky.

So, when you buy a car, ask if you can use lead-free gasoline, *or* if you need regular, high test or extra high test. Then use the one best suited for your auto.

YOUR OWN GOOD MILEAGE

You can help control your car's consumption of gasoline in several important ways. Did you know that stop-and-go driving will consume much more gas than continuous moderate-speed driving on the open road? Also, in colder weather your mileage per gallon is likely to drop. Here are some ways to keep gas mileage as economical as possible:

1. Be sure your car is well tuned and properly adjusted. Do not neglect to service it every 2000 miles.
2. Be sure you are using the proper gasoline for your model car.
3. Keep your tires properly inflated.
4. Use a lighter-weight oil in winter. (Check with your mechanic. He may change your car to a lighter oil automatically.)
5. When driving on the open road, drive as consistently as possible. If the speed limit is 50 mph, drive at a steady speed between 45 and 50. Lags and sudden bursts of speed use up gas.
6. Make sure all filters are periodically cleaned or replaced.
7. Use power options like air-conditioners as seldom as possible.

Checking your mileage. Find out how many miles you are getting per gallon of gasoline and compare it with your auto manual.

To find out if your car passes muster, here's what to do:

1. When you plan a trip, fill up the gas tank and write down the number of miles on your speedometer at the same time.

2. Drive until you need gas again. (See the section on water in the gas, below, for information on when to gas up again.) Fill the tank and note again your speedometer mileage reading and the number of gallons rung up on the gas pump.
3. Subtract this second mileage from the (first) reading you took at the beginning of the trip. This will tell you how many miles you have driven.
4. Now divide the number of gallons of gas used into those miles. This will tell you the miles per gallon.

    For instance

    Mileage at start of trip 14,710
    Mileage at next gas stop 14,790

$$14,790$$
$$-14,710$$
$$\overline{80\text{ miles traveled}}$$

The car takes 5 gallons of gas. $5\overline{)80}^{\,16}$

You are getting 16 miles per gallon.

A SAFETY NOTE

When gassing up, do not smoke, and be sure to turn off the engine. A stray spark could ignite the raw gas.

TERMS AND PHRASES CONCERNING GASOLINE

Water in the gas. Air enters the gas tank and on damp days condenses. The wetness will form at the bottom of the tank because gasoline is lighter than water. You can prevent this by not letting your gas get too low. When you draw gas from the top of the tank you avoid drawing water through the system. Also, the more gasoline in the tank, the less room for air and condensation. So keep the tank between full and half full.

In freezing weather, this same water can freeze, causing ice particles in the gas lines. This can slow or stop the flow of gas to the carburetor. During extremely damp weather, a noncondensing additive can be combined with your gasoline.

Flooding. Too much gasoline and not enough air has entered the carburetor. The car will not start. Wait ten minutes and try again. The cause of the flooding might be a dirty air filter (not enough air getting through), too much fuel-pump pressure, a faulty carburetor float, or even too much pumping on the gas pedal when starting up.

Vapor locks. Extreme heat can evaporate the fuel in the fuel line or fuel pump and cause vapor. As you might imagine, this problem is caused by hot weather, heavy traffic, hard driving, or some combination of the three. The bit of fuel trickling through the lines as the car idles in traffic is brought to a boil and the carburetor becomes starved for fuel.

To help avoid this problem, be sure your cooling system is in good condition (see Chapter 7), or consider having an electronic fuel pump installed.

Backfires. These are popping sounds that usually occur as you release your foot from the accelerator pedal. If your car does this, there could be something wrong. But be aware that certain imported cars, particularly those with high-compression small engines, may backfire because of adjustments made to meet emission control regulations. If your backfiring engine does not fall into this category, its cause may be among the following list of ailments:

1. Heavy deposits of carbon.
2. Unnecessary air leaking into the engine.
3. Burned or sticking valves.
4. Ill-fitting or cracked distributor cap.
5. A fuel-air mixture that is too lean (too much air mixed with the gas).
6. Timing out of adjustment (see Chapter 6).

Consult your mechanic; he may lengthen this list, and he'll help you locate the cause of the backfiring.

Idle. This means the car's engine is running while the car is standing still. It should sound even and smooth. Avoid idling your car unnecessarily. *Never* idle your car in a closed garage.

Misfires. The engine misfires when, after the motor starts and is smoothly chugging, there is a hesitation in the chugs. This could also be called "rough idle" if the car is standing still.

Rough idle. If the car coughs and hiccups as it idles, the adjustment of the idle could be too slow. See your mechanic, since this could also be caused by other problems.

The next time you go for gasoline, you'll have a pretty good idea of what happens to it from the time it enters your tank until it leaves as exhaust. But it might also be a good idea to keep your new small store of knowledge to yourself. After all, you're far from being an expert. Besides, let the mechanic think you're helpless; he can add to your store of knowledge if you just listen to him. You'll also be better able to determine how reliable he is.

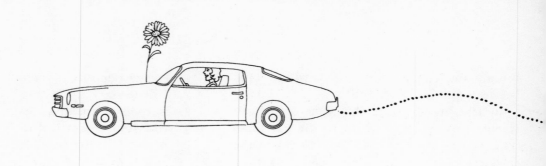

6. THE ELECTRICAL SYSTEM

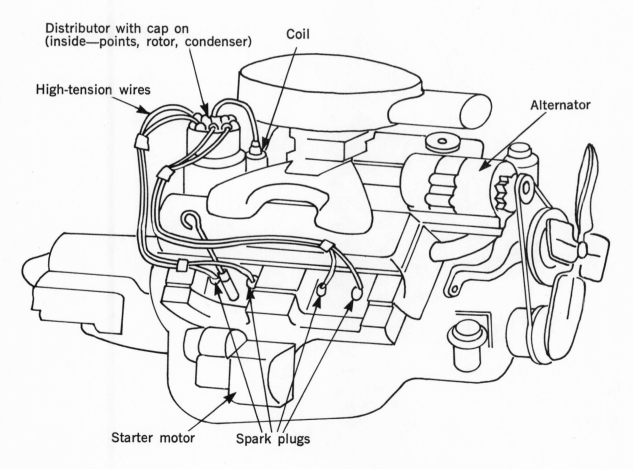

Distributor with cap on
(inside—points, rotor, condenser)

Coil

High-tension wires

Alternator

Starter motor

Spark plugs

I WON'T GO into detail with the complex wiring system of your car, so don't be panicked by the title of the chapter. But to be assured of a well-running vehicle, you need to know how to maintain the battery, what appliances work from the battery, which fuses are which and what they do, and what happens when you turn on the ignition key.

About 80% of your starting problems will be due to faulty electrical adjusting and parts.

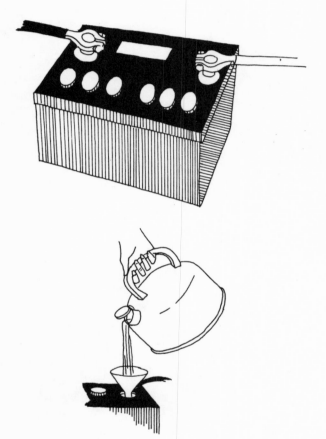

The Battery

Let's start with the battery. That's the very heavy, conservative-looking black box that usually sits in the engine compartment. It's about the size of one of those super four-slice toasters.

As shown in the drawing at left, the caps on the top of the battery can be unsnapped or unscrewed, and distilled water can be carefully poured into the cells (just enough to cover the metal plates inside). I recommend distilled water, because the minerals in tap water often lessen the life of your battery. When you stop for gas, you can have the gas station attendant check the water level and strength of the battery. (Strength refers to the electrolyte level, which determines the liquid's capabilities for conducting electrical current.) *Ask* the attendant to check it, as this is not usually done unless requested. Have the battery checked every two weeks or so, especially in summer, to be sure water has not evaporated from the cells.

You can check the strength of the battery yourself and not have to rely on the gas station attendant. If you suspect that your battery is getting weak (the starter turns sluggishly or the headlights seem dim), you can test the battery with a hydrometer. This instrument looks just like a turkey baster, except that inside the glass tube is a floating scale.

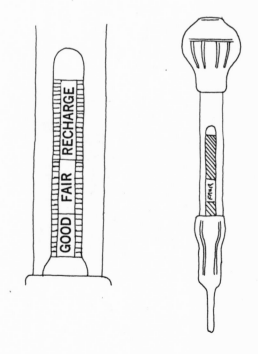

This is how it works:

1. Unscrew or unsnap one of the battery caps.
2. Insert the hydrometer and squeeze the rubber bulb just as though you were picking up juice to baste a turkey. Pull up enough liquid to float the inner glass tube.
3. Lift the water-filled hydrometer out and look at the reading on the floating scale in the glass tube.

Be sure you buy a hydrometer that reads "good," "fair," and "recharge," along with the specific gravity readings. The hydrometer should cost well under $5.00.

The specific gravity scale is a very exact measure of your battery's strength and can be left to your mechanic to interpret. However, the "good," "fair," and "recharge" reading are accurate enough for your needs.

BATTERY CHARGERS

A healthy battery that has become weak from nonuse of the car can usually be rejuvenated by running the engine. However, if your battery is aging and you would like to prolong its use, you can charge it. That is, your gas station attendant (or you, if you care to buy a battery charger) can put a trickle charger on it for a few hours to give it more life. Some gas stations will try to give you a quick, or "hot," ten-minute charge. This can damage your battery. Insist on a trickle charge. (This will take about two hours or more.)

Here is a drawing of how a trickle charger works.

After a few hours of charging, the arrow on the dial of the charger should point to the full charge notation. (Read the directions accompanying the battery charger.) If after the charge the dial reads less than full charge, that's all the life you are going to get from

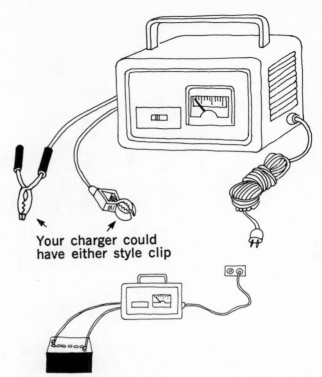

Your charger could have either style clip

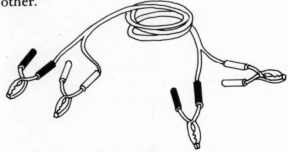

your battery. It may get you through the season, but it will probably need frequent recharging.

JUMPER CABLES

Suppose your car has a weak battery and one morning you find it's dead. Jumper cables, one of the essential pieces of equipment mentioned in Chapter 1, can get you going again. These cables are able to jump the power from the battery of one car to the battery of another.

You will see that your jumper cables have a black and a red clamp at each of the two ends. *This is important!*

39

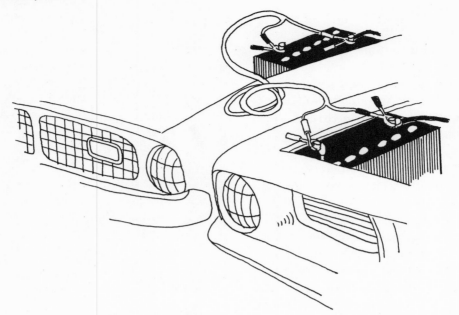

1. Attach the *red* clamp of one end of the jumper to the *red* lead of the battery terminal on your neighbor's car (red to red). (Note: the U.S. auto manufacturer installs a red lead and a black lead in each new car. Sometimes the original red lead is replaced with a black lead by a mechanic. You will recognize this as the actual red, or positive, lead if it leads to the starter motor. Look closely at the battery. Sometimes near the positive post a plus sign is stamped. Red goes to +. The real black, or negative, lead will be attached or grounded onto the engine block, car's frame, or the underside of the fender.) Attach the *black* clamp to the negative (minus sign), or black, lead terminal on your neighbor's car. Mixing negatives and positives could result in a burned out alternator—or at the least, a spectacular display of sparks.

2. Now, with the other ends of the jumper cables, attach red to red and black to black on your own car. Be sure that no other metal connects the two cars. (Bumpers should not touch, and any tow chains should be disconnected.)

3. Have your neighbor start his car. (Be sure you don't work in a closed garage, as the fumes from the cars could be fatal.) Have your neighbor race his engine slightly by depressing the gas pedal. Now try starting your own car. The power from your neighbor's battery should jump to yours and start your engine.

4. Be careful if one of the cars you are dealing with was produced before 1969. Most older cars have generators rather than alternators. Though generators and alternators both serve the same purpose, jumping an alternator car and a generator car could ruin the alternator. To successfully jump with an older car, the battery cables from the car with the healthy battery should be disconnected first.

BATTERY CARE

Keep your battery clean. Grease and battery acid can form on the case and the terminal leads and interfere with good electrical contact. They can be cleaned away with a rag dipped in clear ammonia. Or, paint on a solution of baking soda and water; when the bubbling action starts, wipe it away with a rag. Be careful not to get any of the battery acid on your hands. It can burn you. Do not handle the battery when the motor is running or you could get a good jolt of electricity. Wash your hands with soap and clear water immediately after the cleanup.

When you shop for a new battery, you should know if your car has a six-volt or twelve-volt system. It will most likely have twelve volts. Your garage man can tell you quickly. Don't skimp on cost. Investing in a good battery and taking good care of it can keep you going for three or four years.

The Ignition System

This is what happens when you turn the key and press the starter: two important units

come into effect—the battery and the starter motor. Connecting these two units is a heavy cable that passes through an on/off switch called a solenoid. Aattached to this solenoid are a couple of small wires. One goes to the ignition switch, the other to the ignition coil. The ignition switch also has a wire that attaches to this coil. From the coil a heavy cable runs to the distributor, and from the distributor run cables to each spark plug. Here is a picture of the whole system.

The diagram below is simplified, but I think it gives you an idea of what the ignition's all about.

When your garage man talks of the following items, he will be discussing parts of your ignition system:

Coil	Solenoid
Distributor and cap	Alternator
Points	Spark plugs
Rotor	Voltage regulator
Condenser	Ignition wires
Resistor	Ignition switch
Battery	High-tension wires
Starter motor	

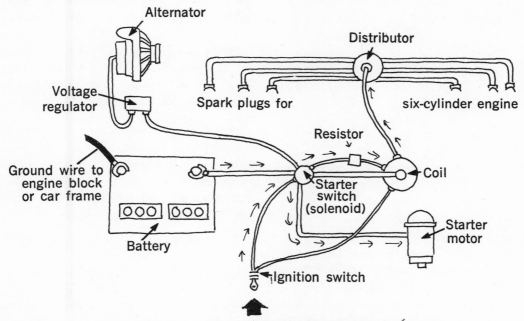

This is a very simplified diagram showing the flow of electrical power from the ignition key to the firing of the spark plugs, which starts combustion

Coil. Electricity travels from your battery along a thick red (positive) cable, eventually reaching the coil. The coil builds up and stores this electricity as the extra voltage

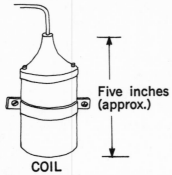

Five inches
(approx.)

COIL

needed for starting and running the engine. It then sends this voltage to the distributor.

Distributor. The distributor distributes the voltage from the coil through the high-tension wires that lead to each spark plug. This causes

DISTRIBUTOR (cap off)

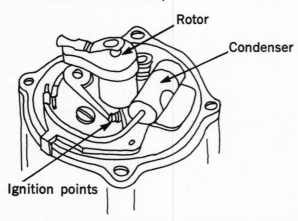

Rotor

Condenser

Ignition points

the plugs to spark in proper sequence and ignites the fuel. (See Chapter 5, page 32.)

Points, rotor, and condenser. These play an intricate part in the distributor's function. They need periodic adjusting or replacing to keep the distributor functioning efficiently.

Resistor. The tiny resistor helps control the amount of voltage going to the coil, which in turn prevents too much electricity from

reaching and burning the spark plug electrodes.

Battery. The battery as a supplier of electricity was explained earlier in this chapter.

Starter motor. The motor that is brought to life by all this electrical voltage is the starter

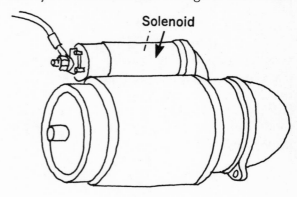

Solenoid

STARTER MOTOR

motor. It is geared to the flywheel, which in turn rotates the engine. (See Chapter 5.)

Starter switch (solenoid). This is the switch that, when unlocked and turned on by your ignition key, activates all preceding functions.

Alternator. This acts like an electric generator. That is, it continues sending electricity back to the battery and keeps the battery alive as the motor runs.

Spark plugs. As mentioned in Chapter 5, the spark plugs ignite the fuel-air vapor sent from the carburetor into the combustion chamber. If you have a four-, six-, or eight-cylinder car, you will have the corresponding four, six, or eight spark plugs. These

must be kept in adjustment or, as they say, "properly gapped." This means that the little metal hook at the base of the plug must be the proper distance from the plug's base. This is where the spark jumps. Your garage man has a tool that will adjust this to the proper distance. The white porcelain portion of the plug must be free of dirt and grease, and because porcelain can break, it must not have any cracks.

Voltage regulator. The battery, alternator, and voltage regulator act as a team to make up the energy for the entire system. The voltage regulator distributes the electrical production of the alternator.

Starting Difficulties

Starting difficulties can, of course, stem from many things, but here are a few common problems particularly related to ignition. One of these could be yours.

1. *Dampness.* Very often, after a heavy rain or prolonged dampness you have difficulty starting your car. Turn off the ignition (always do so when planning to look under the hood unless you really know what you're doing). Open the hood and, with a clean rag, wipe dry the high-tension wires, spark plugs, coil, and distributor cap. This might solve the problem.
2. *Engine turns but will not start.* Perhaps you have forgotten to tromp on the gas pedal as your auto manual recommends. Perhaps the automatic choke won't open (see Chapter 5). If the engine is warm, it could be flooded with too much gasoline. Wait about ten minutes and try again. This is assuming that your car is well tuned and has been running smoothly.

If your car is not well tuned or serviced properly, you may not be getting a strong enough spark from the spark plugs to ignite the fuel-air vapor; or perhaps your ignition timing could be way out of adjustment.
3. *Car won't keep running.* If the engine starts but won't keep running, it could be that the resistor is defective or the ignition wiring damaged. The distributor cap could be cracked, the points could be burned or out of adjustment, the timing could be out of adjustment, wires could be damaged or loose. (This just begins to mention an assortment of problems.) Your ignition system should be completely checked to locate the malfunction. The first thing your mechanic will test is whether you are getting a spark and the strength of that spark.

These are only a few of the many possible ailments your car could be suffering from. Most important for avoiding these ailments is to keep the car in top condition with constant servicing.

Electrical Accessories

Here are some of the accessories that get their power from the battery:

Starter motor	Radio or tape deck
All lights	Clock
(interior and exterior)	Cigarette lighter
Windshield wipers	Horn
Heater fan	Directional signals
Air conditioner	Convertible top
Power windows	

It's a very good idea to turn off all electrical accessories before starting the car. The starter motor needs a good burst of power to activate it, and if the radio is on, the power it takes to operate the radio is lost to your motor.

It's also a good idea to limit your use of accessories in heavy, stop-and-go traffic. This type of driving puts an extra strain on your battery. (The battery doesn't charge much when your car's engine is running at low speeds.)

Fuses or Circuit Breakers

It's important that you know where the fuse (or circuit-breaker) panel is located in your car. It may either be on the dashboard or within the engine compartment.

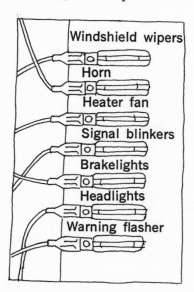

Windshield wipers
Horn
Heater fan
Signal blinkers
Brakelights
Headlights
Warning flasher

These fuses work just the way the ones in your home work. They are safety devices used to cut off the flow of electricity when something in the flow of current is amiss. One fuse may be for the horn and the windshield wipers, another for the headlights, and so on.

Be sure to keep extra fuses on hand. It is likely to be at night when your headlights' fuse blows.

Headlights

The sealed beam has been found to be the most efficient headlight yet devised. Everything—bulb, reflector, lens—is sealed in one unit to stay free from rust and dampness. The bulb will eventually burn out and the entire sealed unit will have to be replaced, but this should not happen for four, five, or even six years.

The dimmer switch on your car converts your headlights from long-distance beams to beams that, when adjusted properly, shine light to the edge of the road. This is espe-

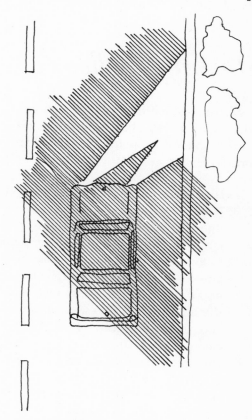

cially valuable when you drive in fog or rain, so be sure this switch is adjusted correctly. Also, be sure your headlights are clean.

It is a courtesy when using the high beams to dip them low when a car approaches from the opposite direction. Then the opposing driver will not be blinded by your headlights' glare, which could cause an accident.

Every once in a while it's a good idea to go over your lighting system. With the help of a companion, check the following:

1. Are both headlights working?
2. Do high and low beams light properly?
3. Are low beams adjusted so that they shine to the edge of the road?
4. Do parking lights work?
5. Do both brakelights work?
6. Do both taillights work?
7. Do the back-up lights work?
8. Do directional signals work?
9. Does the license plate light work?
10. Do the blinking warning lights work?

Gauges and Lights

Most of the newer cars carry what are sarcastically called "idiot lights." Instead of gauges for your temperature, alternator, and oil pressure readings, when trouble occurs a light goes on. Have your mechanic check these lights periodically. You don't know when a bulb may be burned out, and you have no warning of a coming problem before the light goes on—no dial to watch as it gradually creeps up into the trouble zone. When one of these lights goes on, you'd better be on your toes and stop right away. Check your auto manual to see where the lights are located and be sure that they work.

ALTERNATOR LIGHT

This light indicates the discharge of electricity. It is not an immediate danger signal, but it should be checked into as soon as you can. This bulb can light briefly as you start the engine. It is no cause for alarm.

TEMPERATURE LIGHT

This warning light often lights on a summer day when you are in heavy traffic. It means that the coolant in your radiator is hot enough so the warning light goes on. Race the engine for a minute. If the light stays on, pull over to the side, turn off the engine, and let everything simmer down.

If the light goes on for no apparent reason, it may mean that you are low on coolant or that you have a leak somewhere. Look into this immediately. If you suspect that your car is overheated, *never* undo the radiator cap. The pressure inside would send scalding coolant bursting all over you. Wait at least ten minutes before opening the cap. Some cars have a pressure release valve that can be opened to release the steam built up in the radiator under these conditions. For more on these problems, see Chapter 7.

OIL PRESSURE LIGHT

When this lights up it indicates a drop in oil pressure. It does not tell you *how* little pressure there is, so in case it's very little, stop and shut off the engine *immediately*. If there is *no* oil pressure, it means no oil is being circulated through the engine. The engine parts will then heat to such a point that the parts bind. This is very expensive to fix, and the damage could even be beyond repair.

Note that the oil light will glow when you turn on the ignition key, but it should go out shortly after the engine has started.

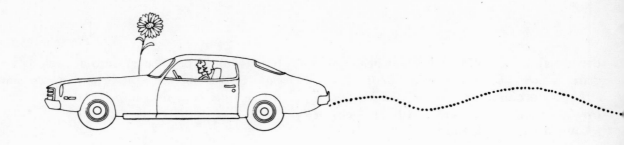

7. THE COOLING SYSTEM

THE WATER-COOLED ENGINE

Within your car are systems specially designed to keep the engine from getting so hot that moving parts bind and movement becomes impossible.

One of these is the cooling system, which incorporates:

Engine block
   (cylinder head)
Radiator and its
   pressure cap
Thermostat

Fan belt, Fan
Water pump
Water hoses
Coolant (water plus
   antifreeze)

The radiator. This is located inside the engine compartment, at the front of the car just behind the front grill. It holds the coolant, a combination of water and antifreeze.

Pumped by the water pump, the coolant circulates from the radiator through the hoses to the engine block. The engine block is the heavy, cast-iron container that holds the inner workings of your engine.

Coolant circulates around the outside of the cylinder chambers. The passages through which this coolant flows are called water jackets. These jackets are located in areas that get particularly hot from the extreme heat of combustion. Because of this, the coolant flowing through these jackets also becomes extremely hot. This very hot coolant is then pumped to the top of the radiator. The radiator cools this heated coolant by passing it through tubes upon which cool air is being blown from the forward thrust of the moving car and the sucking of the fan. Then the whole process starts over again.

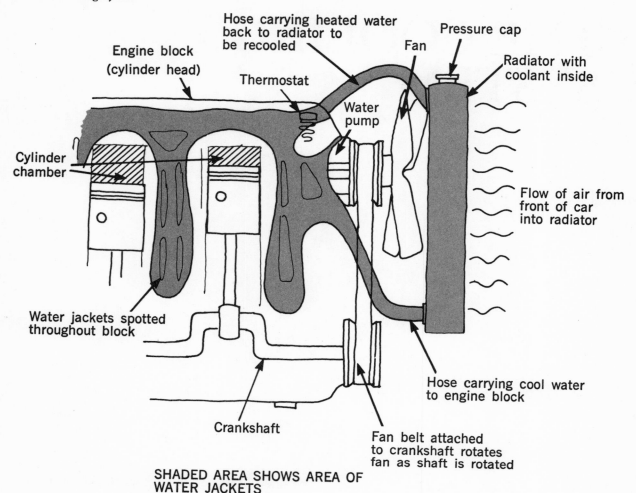

Engine block (cylinder head)

Hose carrying heated water back to radiator to be recooled

Thermostat

Fan

Pressure cap

Radiator with coolant inside

Water pump

Cylinder chamber

Flow of air from front of car into radiator

Water jackets spotted throughout block

Crankshaft

Hose carrying cool water to engine block

Fan belt attached to crankshaft rotates fan as shaft is rotated

SHADED AREA SHOWS AREA OF WATER JACKETS

The thermostat. The thermostat is a small mechanism that regulates the flow of the coolant to the engine block.

Prior to 1968, thermostats used in American autos were designed to open or become effective at 175° to 180°F. Models manufactured after 1968 were designed to open at 195° to 200°F. The thermostat will stay in its closed position until your car warms up and the coolant reaches 195°F., which is your engine's proper operating temperature. Then the thermostat mechanism will automatically open.

In the "closed" position, circulation of coolant is restricted throughout the engine block. Without this coolant, the engine heats

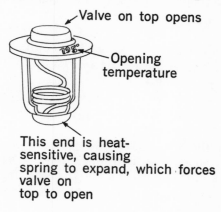

Valve on top opens

Opening temperature

This end is heat-sensitive, causing spring to expand, which forces valve on top to open up rapidly. At 195°F. the thermostat opens, restoring the normal circulation of the coolant in the engine block. It is necessary that the engine be heated quickly so that the oil will be warm enough to flow easily through the engine.

Don't let anyone talk you into running the car without a thermostat so that the car will run cooler. If the thermostat is working properly it couldn't possibly cause the coolant to boil, since the boiling point of your coolant is well above 212°F. Without the thermostat control, the oil throughout your engine is thick, cold, and flows sluggishly for too long a period. This causes sludge deposits to form in the oil passages and results in poor lubrication of vital parts. This could eventually cause big trouble (see Chapter 8).

A secondary function of the thermostat that is most important to your personal comfort is to provide hot water for your heater and defroster ,in winter. Without a thermostat your breath could freeze the windshield and icicles could hang from your tears of frustration.

The fan. The fan is easily located just behind the radiator and looks just like what it's called. Its main function is to keep the coolant cool when there is no air flowing from the car's forward motion. Its effectiveness is at low speeds or at idle. Many fans even disengage at highway speeds.

Be very careful if you decide to investigate this mechanism. *Never* go near it when the engine is running. It has been known to remove fingers. Keep small children away from it. Be careful that nothing drops into the revolving blades, and stand away from the line of trajectory of a blade. If a freak accident occurred (it has been known to) and a blade came loose, the force of the impact could be fatal. *Never* try to rotate the fan by its blades. This can weaken the mechanical parts.

Drive belt. The drive (fan) belt's function is to stretch from one rotating part over to a standing part in order to make this standing part rotate.

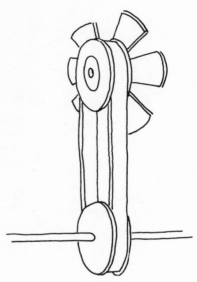

Picture the old-fashioned treadle sewing machine. As you pump the treadle, your action makes a wheel turn. On this wheel is a belt attached to the sewing machine's wheel which makes mechanisms turn, which makes the needle arm go up and down.

In the same way, your fan belt is connected to the crankshaft, which turns because of the engine's combustion (see Chapter 5). The belt is also connected to the fan, causing it to rotate, and usually to the water pump, causing it to pump coolant through the system. It is connected to the alternator (generator), which creates its own electrical supply.

Water pump. The water pump is the main muscle of your cooling system. It pumps the coolant throughout the engine. If it fails, the other functions of the car may also fail.

Radiator pressure cap. The coolant in your radiator boils at a much higher temperature when it is under pressure than it does in an unpressurized system. ·

If your car does overheat, do not inno-

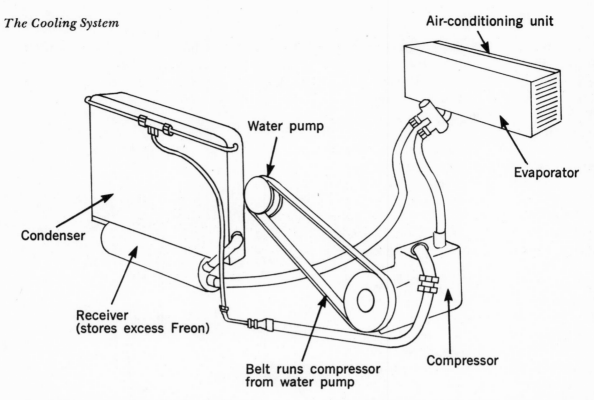

Air-conditioning unit

Water pump

Evaporator

Condenser

Receiver
(stores excess Freon)

Belt runs compressor
from water pump

Compressor

cently walk over and undo the radiator cap. It will burst steam in your face, perhaps causing serious injury. Wait ten minutes or more, then take a rag and slowly undo the cap leaning your body well away.

Every pound of pressure applied to the radiator raises the boiling point of the coolant 3°F. Therefore, with a normal boiling point of 212° plus a pressure cap of fifteen pounds, the boiling point of your coolant will be 257°F. With a thermostat of 195°F. and a fifteen pound pressure cap you have a long way to go before the coolant begins boiling.

Water hoses. Because of the pressure built up in your radiator, the water hoses are continually flexing as the cooling mixture is pumped through. These tough hoses take quite a beating. Check them occasionally with your engine at its normal operating temperature (for example, after a twenty-minute run from the supermarket). Be sure there are no pulpy, soft spots or cracked-looking areas. If there are, call it to your mechanic's attention for replacement.

Air conditioners. These hot weather blessings are run off the rotating power of the crankshaft by a belt to the air conditioner's compressor.

You will find that in laboring to run the air conditioner, your engine will use more gasoline. It may idle poorly, and its internal parts may be different. It will handle somewhat more sluggishly because of the additional weight of the unit. But in my mind these are small costs for the big comfort gained by having an air conditioner. Not only are you cool, but because you drive with the windows shut, the noise from parkway traffic is virtually eliminated. Fresh air is cooled and circulated through the system.

Coolant (water plus antifreeze). The big bad guy in your cooling system is that red devil, rust. As time passes, the accumulation of flaking scale and rust can restrict the circulation of coolant, causing the engine to overheat. Therefore, incorporated within most coolants (containing ethylene glycol-base antifreeze) are a rust retarder and various lubricants. Permanent antifreeze is long lasting, but the compounds in it do deteriorate and must be replaced annually.

Years ago the antifreeze was drained out each season and replaced with water for the summer months. Many people still believe you must do this. *Not so!* Using one antifreeze coolant throughout the year is much healthier for the car for all the reasons mentioned above.

Your garage man can test the strength of the antifreeze each autumn before the first freeze. If it is still clean and strong, nothing need be done except to add a can of rust inhibitor and water pump lubrication. If it does not test to proper strength, your garage man will add antifreeze until the necessary protection is reached. "Necessary protection" varies with where you live. For instance: two-thirds antifreeze to one-third water protects you to 60° below zero. Half antifreeze, half water protects you down to 35° below zero. Sounds supercold? Check with your garage man or read the directions on the antifreeze can for the proper proportion for you. Never use pure antifreeze because it congeals to a jelly in extreme cold.

A MAINTENANCE CHECKLIST

1. Check for wear on all hoses; water hoses, air-conditioner hoses, and heater hoses.
2. Have even the tiniest radiator water leak repaired right away.
3. Check radiator pressure cap for rust and wear. It should fit snugly.
4. Be sure a good quality antifreeze is in your car and is checked for strength each autumn.
5. Know that the thermostat is functioning properly. Ask your service man to check it.

If overheating problems do develop, look for them here:

1. Fan belt is slipping.
2. Radiator is low on coolant.
3. Water is not circulating properly through the system or through the hoses, because of rust or clogging.
4. Leaking hoses or hose connections are causing loss of coolant.
5. Thermostat is malfunctioning.
6. Exterior of radiator is clogged with dust, insects, or dried leaves and grass.
7. Water pump fails.

If when you're on the road, your radiator does boil:

1. Pull over and turn off the engine.
2. Open the hood to help cool it . . . and wait.
3. Aften ten minutes have passed and the gurgling noises have stopped, cautiously open the radiator pressure cap with a rag. Most pressure caps have a relief valve that releases the steam pressure to the side and down so that you don't have to open the cap on that built-up pressure. Just flip the valve and let the steam escape.
4. If no fresh water is available, start hiking for some.
5. After the engine has cooled, start it and add cold water very gradually *with* the engine running. This can only be done if the cooling system isn't completely empty. If it is empty wait until it has completely cooled before adding anything. Pouring anything cooler than boiling on extremely hot parts could crack them.
6. Drive the car with a half-filled radiator only for short distances. Stop, wait to cool, drive again; stop, wait to cool, and so on.
7. After filling, watch carefully for another temperature rise while driving.
8. See your mechanic as soon as possible.

AIR-COOLED ENGINE

That very popular little import called "the beetle" has an air-cooled engine.

The air-cooled engine depends on a large fan, again run by a belt attached to the crankshaft. Protuberances are cast into each cylinder to draw heat out of the engine, and directional vents are used to direct the fan-cooled air to the engine. The amount of cool air directed is again controlled by a thermo-stat. No coolant other than engine oil is used with this system, so there's no need for any winter-summer treatment or check. Your fan belt is the key to success here, and it's a good idea to carry a spare. If yours is an air-cooled engine, follow your auto manual for maintenance suggestions.

So, for trouble-free cooling, make sure your garage man has checked all the items mentioned, and use your head to keep your cool cool.

8. OIL AND OTHER LUBRICANTS

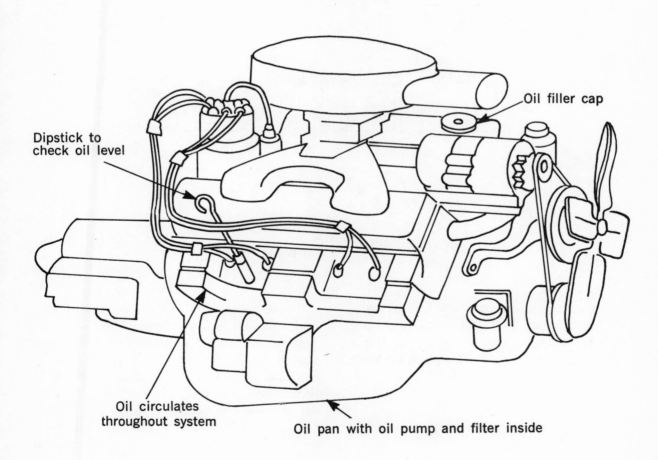

Oil filler cap

Dipstick to
check oil level

Oil circulates
throughout system

Oil pan with oil pump and filter inside

LUBRICATION IS THE distribution of oil and grease throughout the working parts of the engine. A rule of thumb is that oil goes with the engine and grease goes with the chassis.

OIL

When the proper oil is poured into the engine, it flows down to the bottom portion of the engine block, which is called the oil pan. From there it is filtered and pumped throughout the system.

lubricating oil, kerosene, propane, asphalt, to name just a few.

Crude oil is combined with certain compounds to obtain grease. Crude oil is also refined for gasoline engines into different grades and weights.

The oil used for the modern automobile has a great many protecting elements (additives) to guard against rust, wear, and acid formation. It is highly detergent (combines with and suspends foul matter) and has the ability to flow freely in various temperatures. Its free-flowing ability in cold weather is an-

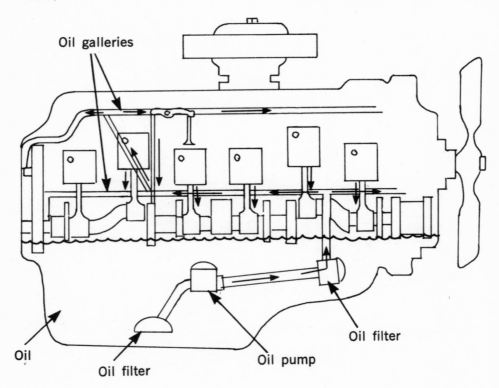

Oil galleries

Oil

Oil filter

Oil pump

Oil filter

Without this lubrication, two metal parts grinding together, back and forth, at a rapid rate cause friction heat of such intensity as to bind these metal parts. Your engine absolutely *cannot* function without this oil lubrication.

Grades of oil. Many products are refined from crude oil from beneath the ground: gasoline,

other consideration. An oil is needed that will function properly when the engine is both at its coldest and hottest. The oil is graded by its viscosity, with a number 10 grade as the thinnest and number 40 grade the thickest. The faster an oil flows, the thinner and the less viscous it is.

Consult your auto manual or your mechanic, and learn the type of oil best suited to your car. Then if you need oil in strange territory, you will know what to ask for.

Oil changing. Your oil will need changing periodically. Read your auto manual. A schedule something like the following is usually recommended for normal changing.

1. *Long-distance driving with little stop and go:* change oil every 4000 miles.
2. *Stop-and-go driving in town or city:* change oil every 2000 miles (in cold weather change more frequently—every 1000 to 1500 miles).
3. *Driving in hot weather on dirt roads:* change oil every 500 miles.

You might want to add a can of STP, Wynns, or Bardahl every 6000 miles or so. These additives have a special coating ability that helps the oil cling to engine parts.

Your auto manual may recommend a change from winter to summer. Ask your mechanic, because if you are using a multi-viscous oil, it may be used all year long. This oil varies in thickness according to the weather and will flow freely whatever the temperature. The can will probably be labeled as 10–30 or 10–40.

Oil filters. Again, read your auto manual to find out when to change the oil filter. Many people feel it should be changed every other oil change.

Engine breather caps. Be sure your mechanic cleans the engine breather caps when a new oil filter is installed. These breathers help dispel unhealthy oil fumes and debris that could do harm to the engine.

Check your oil. You can easily check to see if you have enough oil in your car right in your own driveway. In the engine there are usually two dipsticks. One is for the engine oil, and the other is for the automatic transmission

fluid. They look like this. Your finger goes through the hole to lift out the stick.

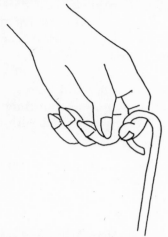

After turning off your engine, wait ten minutes before checking, so the oil can drain back into the oil pan. Make sure your car is level. If you are facing uphill or downhill, you will not get an accurate reading.

The dipstick that goes directly into the engine block (the big mass of iron that houses all the inner workings of the engine) is the one you want to use to check the engine oil. Here are the steps to follow after the engine has cooled and the engine has drained back into the oil pan:

1. Lift the dipstick out of its hole.
2. Wipe it off with a rag.
3. Dip it back into its hole all the way.
4. Lift it out and read the oil level.

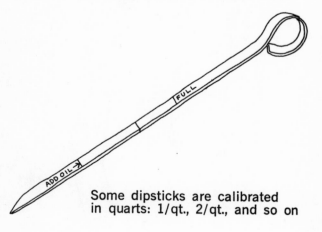

Some dipsticks are calibrated in quarts: 1/qt., 2/qt., and so on

5. Only add oil if it is indicated on the dipstick. Do *not* overfill. This can lead to possible oil-seal damage, but even without this damage the extra oil will burn off in clouds of exhaust from your tailpipe.

The variety of codes and gradings printed on the oil cans became so confusing that the industry has recently come out with a simplified coding:

SE on the can means approved for U.S. cars built after 1971.

SD on the can means for U.S. cars built from 1968–1971.

SC on the can means for U.S. cars built from 1964–1967.

Have your mechanic advise you for any U.S. auto built before 1964.

Adding oil. Look for a capped funnel within the engine (see illustration below). Your garage man will remove this cap, jam a pouring spout onto the oil can, and tip the can into the oil filler.

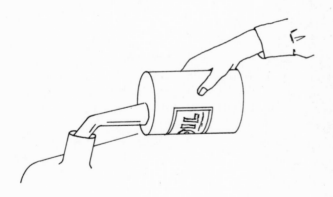

Automatic transmission oil or fluid. The oil lubricant used in the automatic transmission is of a much finer quality than that used in the engine. Naturally, it costs more. There is a dipstick for checking this oil, and on some cars it must be changed occasionally. Leave this checking and changing to your mechanic, but read your auto manual to become familiar with the type of lubricant recommended.

GREASE

I'm sure you've heard the expression "the car needs a grease job" often enough. Pay attention to the phrase. It's an important one.

Grease is about the same consistency as Vaseline and is used to lubricate the chassis, wheel bearings, universal joints, and other mechanical parts outside the engine. But each of these parts takes a different type of grease. If your car begins to whistle and sing with various squeals and squawks, you have been neglecting the grease. If you continue to neglect it, bad trouble can develop. Your steering could fail or brakes not function, and this is only mentioning two critical situations.

For proper maintenance, some mechanics recommend that the car be greased every 2000 to 3000 miles in spite of what some manufacturers suggest. Do not neglect your mechanic's advice.

PARTS TO LUBRICATE

Steering box
Speedometer cable
Windshield-wiper mechanism
Door and trunk locks
Door and trunk hinges
Hood latch

Parking brake mechanism
Telescoping radio antenna
Station wagon tailgate hinges
Just about anything that moves

So that you can check to see when your car was last serviced, the garage usually puts a sticker on the door's edge showing the mileage and what was done at that time. Subtract the mileage noted from your present speedometer reading to get the number of miles you have traveled since your car was last serviced.

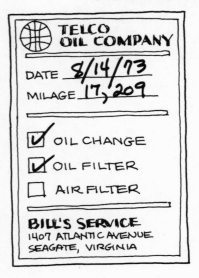

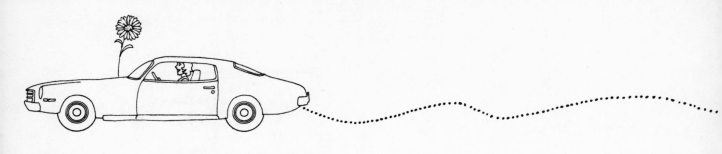

.....9. THE BRAKES

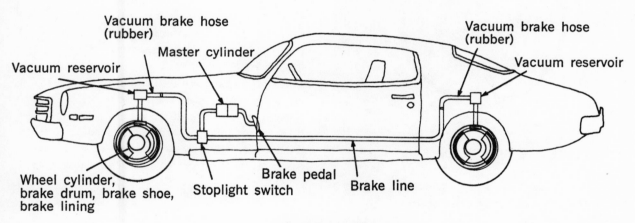

Vacuum brake hose
(rubber)

Master cylinder

Vacuum reservoir

Vacuum brake hose
(rubber)

Vacuum reservoir

Wheel cylinder,
brake drum, brake shoe,
brake lining

Stoplight switch

Brake pedal

Brake line

POWER BRAKES

HOW THE BRAKES WORK

These items make up your brake system:

Master cylinder	Brake drums
Hydraulic fluid	Brake linings
Brake pedal	Brake shoes
Wheel bearings	Wheel cylinder

Because of them this simple action is possible: 1. Step on brake. 2. Stop the car.

Mounted on each wheel of your car is a brake drum. Inside this drum are the brake shoes. Between the drum and the shoe and mounted on the shoe are the brake linings. When you step on the brake, the nonrotating brake shoe expands, pressing the brake shoe with its lining very hard against the rotating drum. This is what stops the rotating motion of the drum (and the wheel and the tire).

Brakes, which are incorporated into all four

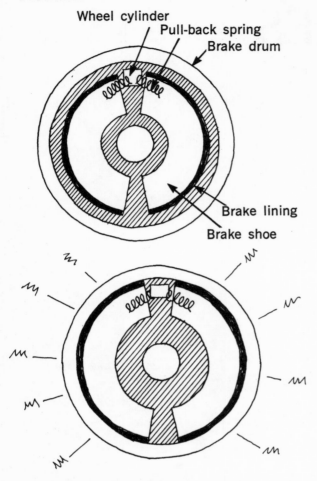

Wheel cylinder
Pull-back spring
Brake drum
Brake lining
Brake shoe

BRAKE MECHANISM INSIDE EACH WHEEL

wheels, are hydraulically operated, using brake fluid for the hydraulic action.

When you press your foot on the brake pedal:

1. The master cylinder pumps hydraulic fluid through pipes and feed lines to the four wheels of the car.
2. On each wheel is a wheel cylinder, which fills with fluid as pressure is built up from the pumping master cylinder.
3. The miniature piston inside the wheel cylinder is forced into motion, causing the brake shoes to be moved outward, pressing the brake linings against the drum.

When you release the brake pedal, heavy springs in the drum relax the brake shoe, causing the fluid to be forced back into the master cylinder.

Since 1966, U.S. autos have come equipped with a divided, or dual, master cylinder. If the fluid drains out of half the cylinder, you still can depend on the other half. One section controls the front wheels, the other the back. Of course, the cylinder should be checked, and the fluid replaced, as soon as possible.

POWER BRAKES

These brakes function no differently than hydraulic brakes. The only addition is a vacuum reservoir, or power brake unit. This unit is connected to the engine by a vacuum hose. It uses the vacuum built up in the engine to help apply pressure to the brake pedal and thus achieves better braking with less effort.

Power brakes are extremely effective. If, in an emergency, you slam them on, all your passengers could end up in the front seat. Be forewarned. Power brakes take some getting used to, so practice with your new car on a quiet street, and get to know just how they'll react.

DISC BRAKES

Many U.S. autos and most imports come equipped with disc brakes on the front wheels. Instead of using a brake drum, a disc is used with a brake lining pad on each side of the disc. This pad replaces the shoe and lining. When the brake pedal is pressed, the pads are squeezed against the rotating disc by means of a hydraulically operated pincer.

These brakes are very effective. Power-assist is almost mandatory, and since these brakes give little indication that they are be-

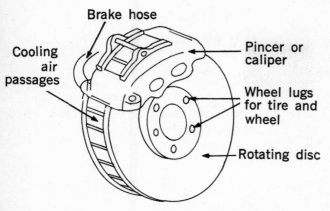

coming seriously worn, they should be checked periodically.

PARKING (HAND) BRAKE

The parking brake works mechanically rather than hydraulically. It uses the same brake drums and shoes as the foot pedal, but it is connected only to the rear wheels. Instead of hydraulic fluid opening the shoes against the drum, mechanical cables open the shoes.

Do not ignore this brake. If your hydraulic brakes should ever fail, the hand brake could save your life. Though it will be many, many yards before it stops the car, it will eventually stop it.

Use the hand brake when you park. Leaving your automatic transmission car in the "park" position alone only puts a strain on the parking unit in the transmission. You should use both the park position and the hand brake. And leaving your standard transmission car in gear without the brake puts a strain on the meshed gear teeth. If someone did give you a bump, this could tear a couple of those teeth out. (Expensive.)

SERVICE AND MAINTENANCE

1. Be sure you have enough hydraulic brake fluid in the master cylinder. Have this checked every 1000 miles.

2. Be sure your mechanic is aware of the condition of the brake linings and drums and that these fit properly. Have them checked once each year.
3. The wheel cylinders should be clean, the protective rubber cups within fresh, and the shoe lubricated.
4. The brake lines should be in good condition with no corrosion.

TROUBLE-SHOOTING YOUR BRAKES

1. If you press the brake, and it slowly sinks to the floor, tell your mechanic so he can find the problem. It could be a leak in the master cylinder. The pedal should stay firm when pressed to its limit.
2. A stain or fluid on the garage floor by the wheels or on the inside walls of the tire could mean trouble with the wheel cylinder.
3. Normal brake pedal action with poor braking power amid squawks and squeals probably means new brake linings are necessary. Worn linings can also damage the brake drums.
4. After heavy rain or flooding, test your brakes. If they do not grab, pump the pedal lightly. This friction should dry out the soaked linings.
5. After overnight parking in very cold weather your emergency brake can freeze in the "on" position. Normal engine warm-up could soon thaw it enough to release it, but if not, try moving the car very gently back and forth and applying the brake more firmly. If this doesn't work, wait till the sun comes up.
6. If the brakes grab or pull to the side, have them checked right away.
7. A "spongy" pedal could indicate air in the brake lines. A mechanic must "bleed," or draw, this air out.

STOPPING POWER

Here are frequently recommended following distances necessary when you travel at a specified number of miles per hour. Note this listing and remember, DO NOT TAIL-GATE!

At 10 miles per hour—20 feet.
At 30 miles per hour—60 feet.
At 60 miles per hour—120 feet.

This list applies only to good driving conditions on dry pavements. (See Chapter 14 for driving in bad conditions.)

10. THE EXHAUST SYSTEM

THE EXHAUST SYSTEM of your car removes the wastes caused by combustion and helps muffle excess noise. Here are some of its parts:

Exhaust manifold   Resonator
Exhaust pipes   Tailpipe
Muffler   Brackets

EXHAUST MANIFOLD

After engine combustion (see Chapter 5), the exhaust manifold opens to expel the exhausted gases through the proper channels. The heat riser valve, when heated by the ex-

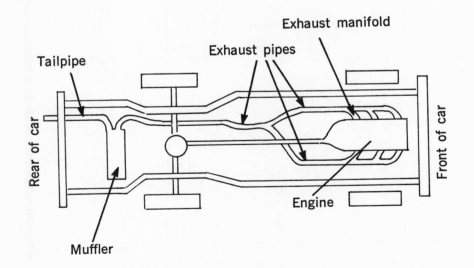

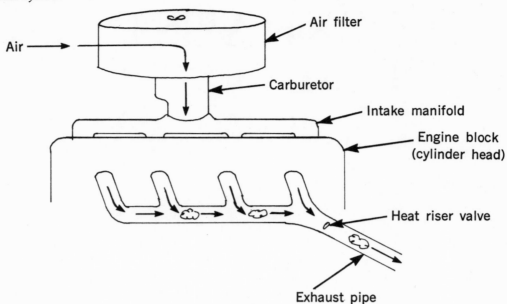

haust manifold, opens the path to emit these waste gases. This valve must be checked by a mechanic to be sure it is lubricated and working freely. Wear can cause the valve mechanism to loosen on the exhaust manifold, letting carbon monoxide fumes into the car's passenger compartment. As this can happen without your knowledge, always drive with some ventilation, even in the coldest weather.

EXHAUST PIPES

These pipes connect the exhaust manifold with the muffler. The exhaust gases pass along this pipe, and if there is any corrosion or cracking in the pipe, you will start to hear an increasing roar from your engine. These pipes are better replaced than mended. If there is rust in one area, other areas will soon be rusting too.

MUFFLER

The exhaust travels through the exhaust pipes to the muffler. The muffler's function is to quiet the din of the exhaust. The muffler is usually made of a galvanized metal to protect it from corrosion. Since it is located beneath the car, you can imagine the amount of rain, splash, snow-melting chemicals, and dirt that the muffler must survive. If you cut the muffler in half you will find a couple of baffles inside, each of which is designed to quiet the noise yet let the exhaust gases pass through freely.

If the muffler has corroded through its surface (this often starts with a small peanut-sized hole), you will begin to hear the distinct pam-pam-pam of the engine. This hole will get progressively worse, sometimes within days, sometimes within weeks, until your car sounds like a Sherman tank. Forget about having it mended. If there is corrosion, chances are a new hole will develop next to the mend. Be sure to replace the muffler with one designed for *your* car. Too small a muffler or one with too few baffles can lead to all sorts of complications: rattles, noise, or improper expelling of the gases.

Be careful if you find you've driven over a large bump and have hit bottom. Aside from damaging the oil pan (bad news) you could have put a crimp in the muffler or kinked the exhaust pipe. Better let your mechanic take a look. Improper exhaust emission can be dangerous and, in most states, illegal.

RESONATOR

This is a small, additional muffler that is installed in some cars to give your car an even quieter hum.

TAILPIPE

This is the final extension pipe that sticks out the back of the car. Sometimes it is a plain, old, grubby-looking pipe, and sometimes it will have a shiny chrome cover on it. The fumes come out of the tailpipe.

Once, while backing out of a tight spot, I nudged the car against a grassy embankment. As I drove away, I noticed that the car made a hollow wa-wa-wa sound instead of its usual rum-rum-rum. I got out to look around the back and saw a big clod of mud and sod clogging the tailpipe. Look out for this sort of thing. If something like this happens, exhaust fumes could back up in the system.

BRACKETS

The exhaust system is supported by a series of brackets that prevent the system from contacting the car's body. Aside from avoiding an annoying clank against the body, these brackets prevent the sparks that might result if a metal part of the exhaust system clanked with the metal of the body—possibly causing a fire. These support brackets can corrode and must be inspected for possible need for replacement.

DUAL EXHAUST

Some manufacturers install a dual-exhaust system (two of everything, one of each on either side of the car) to their large eight-cylinder engine models. It is not reasonable to have your car converted from single to dual or vice-versa. The manufacturer has a team of highly paid engineers who, through knowledge and experiment, have developed your exhaust system. Don't let a backyard mechanic convince you that you'll save gas by converting. Keep what you have and replace parts with the correct new parts.

CARBON MONOXIDE

Only a minor part of the exhaust system is devoted to the comfort of a quietly running engine. The most important function is to dispel the noxious gases away from your car. If a large amount of lethal, odorless carbon monoxide escapes into the driving compartment, you will be killed. A less than lethal amount can make you very ill or put you to sleep at the wheel. Don't play games with your exhaust system. Have it checked often, and don't neglect repairs.

EXHAUST EMISSION SYSTEMS AND GOVERNMENT CONTROLS

There has been recent public disclosure of the poisons produced in automobile emissions. It has been said that an average car expels enough poison in its lifetime to kill the population of a fair-sized city.

All cars sold in the United States have certain emission control systems, but these have been found to be not nearly effective enough. The federal government has established dates by which all manufacturers must have even more effective controls.

11. THE STEERING AND SUSPENSION

STEERING

Following are some of the parts involved in or related to the steering mechanism of your car:

Steering wheel
Steering column
Steering gear box
Sector shaft and
    Pitman arm
Tie rod

Tie rod adjustment
Steering knuckle
Idler arm
Tie rod end
Steering arm

When you move the steering wheel, the steering shaft within the steering column moves in the steering box. The gears in this box reduce the amount of effort you must use to steer. A series of linkages including the

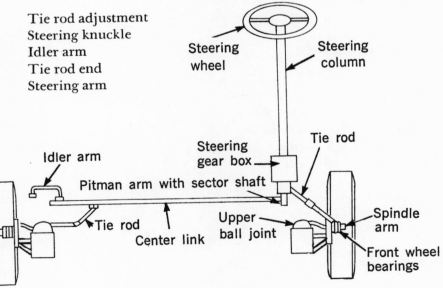

FRONT WHEELS AND STEERING

67

Pitman arm, center link, idler arm, tie rods, ball joints, sector shaft, and tie rod ends, send the steering motion from the gear box to the front wheels.

Steering adjustments are very critical, and the sophisticated machines used to align them are a must in a modern garage.

WHEEL ALIGNMENT

The alignment of your wheels is most important to proper steering.

There are three important adjustments:

1. Camber.
2. Caster.
3. Toe-in (or out).

Camber. Camber is the normal tilt of the wheel of your particular car as you face the car, looking at its front.

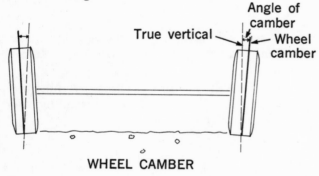

WHEEL CAMBER

This adjustment keeps the wheels in proper contact with the roadway. It is effective when riding on a road with a high crown or on one that slants from the center to the shoulders. When rounding a corner, this adjustment holds your wheels true to the road surface.

If the adjustment is improper, your tires will wear unevenly. The tires would also be apt to squeal on turns and corners.

Caster. Caster creates road stability and ease in steering. The front wheels of a car are adjusted from true vertical to the direction of the steering axis. This is called the caster

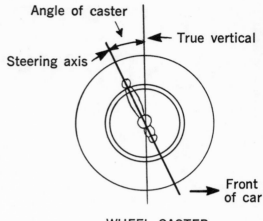

WHEEL CASTER

angle. It cannot be seen by just looking at the wheel, as it is a minute adjustment.

Toe in (or -out). The result of an excessive amount of toe-in or toe-out of the wheels can scuff the tires down the street at an angle and rip off the tread. The tie rods should be properly adjusted to avoid this fault. These rods

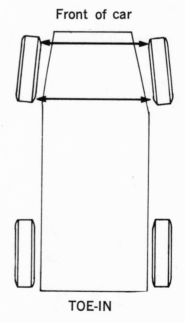

TOE-IN

can be bent in an accident, causing toe-in or toe-out. This drawing is exaggerated so don't try to see this angle by squinting at your own front wheels.

With poor toe-in adjustment, the tires will become scuffed within 300 or 400 miles and will be likely to squeal on corners.

Steering linkages. Steering linkages are all the involved connections, arms and links, that help make up the steering system. It is very important to lubricate steering linkages to avoid wear. This is part of the maintenance that should be included in your 2000-mile grease job (see Chapter 8). These linkages are all susceptible to wear.

Power steering. Power steering is almost a must on today's cars. The ease with which you can steer, particularly in city or town driving, makes it worth the extra cost. If you are buying a little economy car, it won't be necessary, but it makes any of the standard-sized cars easier to handle. There is some additional maintenance, and should the power system fail, steering can become more than normally difficult.

However, the power steering unit has been well developed and should give you little trouble. One danger sign is when hydraulic power steering fluid stains your parking place. How do you know the stain is power steering fluid? You don't. But any stain that reappears should be investigated.

The belt from the engine that helps drive the power steering must be in good condition and its tension properly adjusted. If this belt is out of adjustment you could squeal or quiver when you turn a sharp corner. There are belt dressings on the market that can be squirted on the belt if the squealing persists even after adjustments.

Wheel bearings. The wheel hubs rotate on roller wheel bearings. These bearings must be periodically inspected for wear, cleaned, and repacked with grease. A worn wheel bearing can make a variety of different noises in the wheel affected. Tightening, maintaining, or replacing these wheel bearings should be done by an experienced mechanic.

SUSPENSION

The suspension system of your car consists of the following items:

Frame	Torsion bars
Shock absorbers	(on some cars)
Coil springs	Ball joints
Leaf springs	Stabilizer bar

Without a suspension system your car and you would become battered and bruised by bumps and holes in the road. You would have to be tied down to the seat to keep from flying up and hitting your head on the ceiling. At high speeds the car would be totally unmanageable. Therefore, the body of the car is suspended by springs and shock absorbers to protect you from the rattling and jarring that your wheels most suffer.

Shock absorbers. There are at least four shock absorbers in the car, one for each wheel. They are usually actuated by hydraulic fluid, and they create a restricting action that reduces the powerful bounce of the springs. Without them you might resemble a giant pogo stick as you spring down the highway. If the shock absorbers become defective, you could experience total lack of control of your car. (Have you ever tried to steer a pogo stick at fifty miles an hour?)

If the front of your car bounces more than once after a sudden stop, see your mechanic. Shock absorbers should be checked periodically, anyway. They should be replaced, not repaired, and they should be replaced in pairs so that the bounce control is balanced on both sides of the car.

Springs. The body of your car is hung from the springs. There are three types of springs most commonly used by U.S. manufacturers: coil springs, leaf springs, and torsion bars.

Some autos have coil springs all around, and some have leaf springs at the rear and

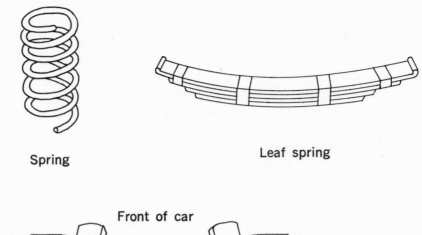

Spring

Leaf spring

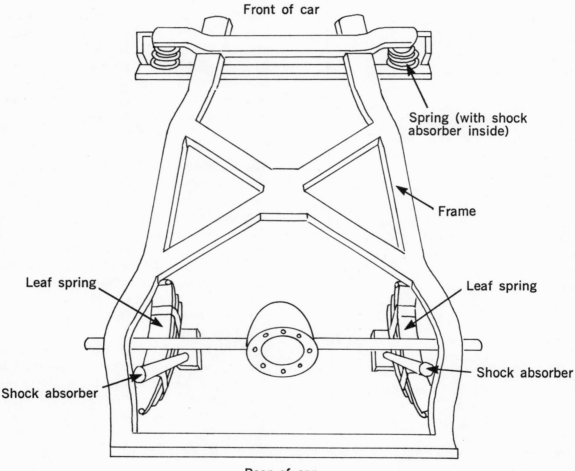

Front of car

Spring (with shock absorber inside)

Frame

Leaf spring

Leaf spring

Shock absorber

Shock absorber

Rear of car

coil springs at the front. Some have torsion bars in the front and coil or leaf springs in the rear. Which spring is best? There is no proof that one is better than another for general driving. If you plan to carry heavy loads, tow a boat or trailer, heavier suspension or a "load-leveling device" can be installed in your car.

Ball joint linkages. Another important point of lubrication is the ball joint linkages. Without lubrication or with wear, these linkages can separate from their sockets and leave you with a complete loss of steering, or perhaps with loss of the affected wheel. Therefore, lubrication is as important as the inspection of these linkages for wear at the time of lubrication.

Independent suspension. Wheels are not mounted on a solid, rigid axle. Instead, each wheel is individually suspended so that each wheel can bounce up and down without affecting the whole car.

Maintaining the suspension system. Be sure that your mechanic has greased all linkages and connections and examined them for wear.

Be aware of any peculiar noises. The wheels may not be properly mounted, the wheel bearings may be worn, or the steering may be out of adjustment. It might be something simple like a stone jammed into the tire tread that is making a rhythmic clickety-click. It could be loose gravel or pebbles in the hubcap or a loose lug nut if the noise is like a couple of Mexican huarachas. Don't ignore *any* wheel noise. Even if it turns out to be just a pebble, you will at least know you're not in big trouble.

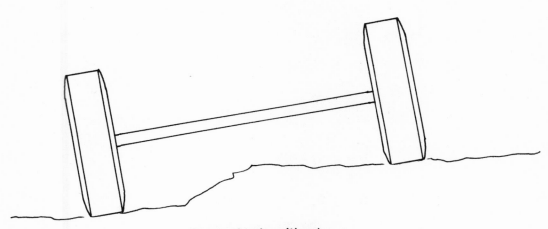

Front wheels without
independent suspension

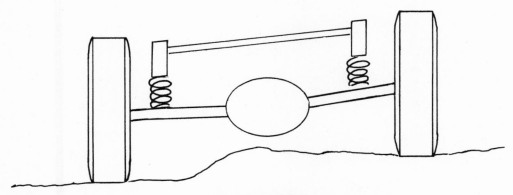

Front wheels with
independent suspension

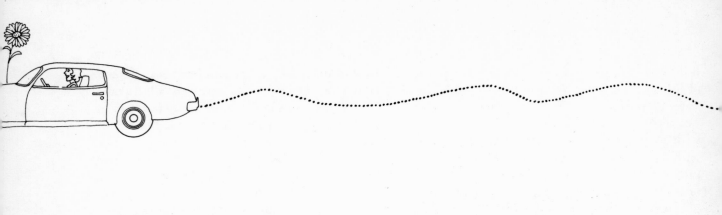

12. THE TRANSMISSION AND REAR AXLE

The Transmission

The large number of parts and the complexities of the parts make it impossible to go into this mechanism in all its technical detail without devoting many pages to it. But we can discuss the transmission as simply as possible and locate its position.

Many people haven't the foggiest notion of what the function of the transmission is. What does it do? For an example, picture a two-wheel bicycle. Pressure on the pedals rotates a gear sprocket. The rotation of this large sprocket moves the chain along to a smaller sprocket at the rear and to the rear wheel. Thus with each pedal rotation you will have

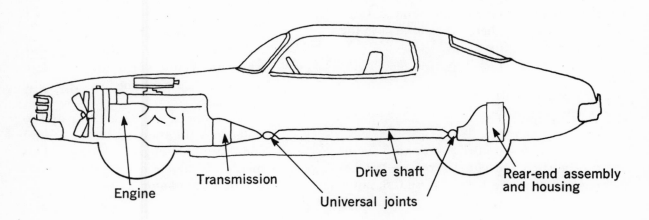

Engine   Transmission   Universal joints   Drive shaft   Rear-end assembly and housing

two wheel rotations. Without this you would be wasting a great deal of effort in your ratio of rapid pedaling to wheel rotation. Your bike may have a gearshift to help you if you want to pedal up a steep hill. When you shift the bike into a lower gear, your ratio changes to one pedal rotation for one wheel rotation, thus making your climb much less exhausting.

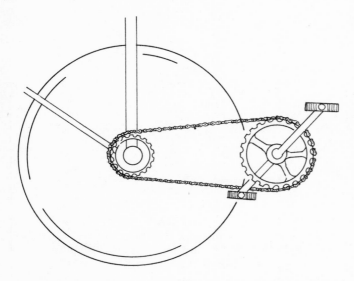

Your auto's transmission is much like the two-wheeler. When your car labors up a hill you also develop more power by shifting to a low gear. This forces the engine to turn more rapidly. Thus, even though the wheels are turning more slowly than on the level highway, their spinning motion is much more forceful because of the engine's rapid turning. The wheels are therefore able to push the car with more strength.

THE MANUAL TRANSMISSION

If you know how to drive a car with standard transmission and clutch, you are fast becoming one of a rare breed. Most U.S. autos

with manual or standard transmission have four forward gear choices and one for reverse; low or first for starting, second and third for acceleration, high or fourth for normal driving over 40 mph, and reverse for backing up. There is also a clutch that must be pressed downward and held while changing these gears. Changing gears without pressing the clutch would most likely rip off a lot of the teeth from the gears. The clutch, then, is the mechanism that, in principle, equalizes the movement of the gears so that the teeth interlock with one another.

AUTOMATIC TRANSMISSION

With automatic transmission, clutch and shifting become obsolete. All the shifting of gears is done automatically by the inclusion of many sophisticated parts within the transmission.

Automatic transmission repairs can be one of the most expensive on your car so preventive maintenance is very important. The transmission should be serviced thoroughly every 10,000 to 15,000 miles. The transmission oil level (see Chapter 8) should be checked each time the engine oil is checked because heat is one of the greatest enemies. If the oil level is low, add the proper oil and have your mechanic find out *why* the level became low.

In order to extend the life of your transmission, here are some rules to follow:

1. Avoid low oil levels.
2. Never put the car in drive or reverse when the engine is running very fast. Let your engine resume its normal idle speed first.
3. When stopped in heavy, stop-and-go traffic, put the transmission in neutral and run the engine slightly. This speeds up the circulation of the coolant in the radiator.

4. Check your driving manual for when to change transmission oil.

5. Avoid extensive rocking by switching from low to reverse to low to reverse when stuck in mud or snow.

6. Avoid screech-away starts.

7. Beware of having your car towed. To eliminate the possibility of a tow ruining the transmission, the rear wheels should be raised from the ground or the drive shaft should be disconnected. (On front-wheel drive the front wheels should be raised.) The mechanic towing you will disconnect this.

8. Avoid holding one foot on the brake and the other on the accelerator. This generates heat, which can ruin both systems.

9. Avoid letting the car sit with the engine running for long periods of time. Some cars have parts that are not lubricated when idling.

10. Avoid starting up immediately in cold weather. Give the transmission fluid a chance to warm up (along with other engine lubricants).

The passing gear. This gives you an extra bolt of power for passing or getting out of an emergency situation. Many people are unaware of the existence of the passing gear which is built into most automatic transmissions. This gear is activated by tromping the accelerator pedal to the floor and then backing off on it.

Creepage. Most autos with automatic transmissions tend to creep forward when idling at a traffic light while in gear. Therefore, light pressure must be kept on the brake pedal. This creeping motion is quite normal, but if the creep ever seems more than you usually experience, your engine could be run-ning faster than recommended at idle speed. Have your mechanic adjust this.

Be aware of any change in the noise level or feel of the transmission. See your mechanic about any grinds, shudders, or jerks when the transmission shifts. In other words, drive by the seat of your pants.

The Rear Axle

Listed here are some of the parts of your rear axle:

Drive shaft	Driving gear
Universal joints	Axle shafts or drives
Rear axle housing and assembly	Differential

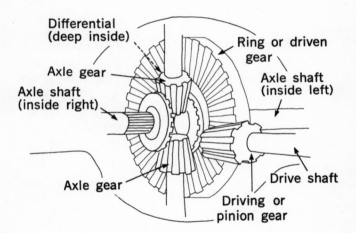

Drive shaft with universal joints. The drive shaft revolves from the transmission through a series of universal joints to the rear axle assembly.

The universal joints allow the drive shaft to shift up and down with the humps and bumps in the roadway. If a universal joint is worn badly, the car will vibrate and clank when slowing down or speeding up. Have this repaired quickly to avoid more serious trouble.

Rear axle housing and assembly. The rear axle housing, as you might imagine, is the enclosed nest in which all the gearing and mechanism to rotate the rear wheels are contained. The lubricant within this housing must be checked both for level and condition.

Ring gear. This is the large gear within the rear axle assembly that rotates the two axle shafts and wheels.

Driving (or pinion) gear. The drive shaft terminates in the pinion gear, which when rotating, engages with the ring gear.

To summarize: from crankshaft—to transmission—to drive shaft—to driving gear—to ring gear—to axle—to the wheels.

Axle shafts. These rotating bars connect the transmission to the wheel.

Differential. You've probably noticed that when you steer a car only the front wheels turn. The back wheels sort of tag along. Now

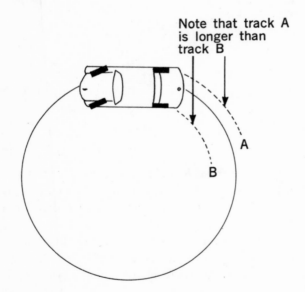

Note that track A is longer than track B

observe that when you turn to the left, the outside rear wheel must travel further and therefore, to keep up, faster than the right wheel.

To accommodate this need, the left wheel is rotated by one axle shaft and the right by another. If these two separate axles were one axle from wheel to wheel, the tires would scuff and drag on the roadway when you turn the car.

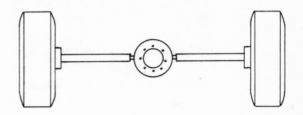

The differential, located deep inside the rear axle assembly, controls the rotating speed of the two axles. When the car is going straight ahead, the gears within the differential remain unengaged. But when you turn, these gears engage in order to control the speed of each of the rear wheels individually.

Limited slip differential. This is an optional device that is valuable in snowy, muddy, or icy conditions. The limited slip differential cancels the action of the differential in slippery conditions, thus "limiting the slip."

So the simple rear axle is not so simple after all. Treat it kindly by servicing it with grease and inspection whenever your car is greased.

13. BUYING YOUR DREAM CAR

BUYING YOUR DREAM car is a very personal thing. Though I'll say, "be practical," don't be *too* practical. If you're a lighthearted person, just because it rains a lot and you have four kids and a big dog, you really don't have to buy a cumbersome gray station wagon. And if you're pretty and have flirtatious eyes and an adventurous spirit, you will not ruin your image if you really don't want the low, red roadster. If color is important to you, don't compromise if you can possibly avoid it. Get the color you want. A car is a big investment and you'll never be happy with a second- or third-choice color.

But let's take the practical side. If you drive thirty miles to work each day on a high-speed highway, you will be much better off *not* driving a little compact. Definitely, for your own comfort and safety, look into a heavier car. If price is a problem, Plymouth, Chevrolet, Ford, and AMC put out less expensive middleweights.

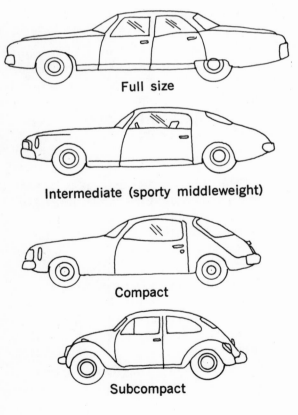

Full size

Intermediate (sporty middleweight)

Compact

Subcompact

If you fall madly in love with "Acme Motors'" new little "Bob Cat," wait a year. Let it prove itself.

If you have a gigantic, floppy-eared dog who gets earaches, or if you have a sinus problem, stay away from convertibles. And though it's nice to imagine the breezes rippling through your hair, there's usually a gale wind in a convertible. Your hair won't ripple, it will tangle and knot. So if hair is a concern, don't consider the open car.

At one time you had the choice of two-door, four-door, vinyl top, convertible, station wagon, hard top, and van. Now some manufacturers are trying to combine all the assets of the above cars into one versatile car for all people. The top of this car slides back to open for a sunroof and the back seat flops down for carting. The trunk opens to give access to the flattened-out seat area like a station wagon. It's really very neat.

ACCESSORIES

Now that you know what model you want, find out exactly what accessories come within the price you choose. Anything additional is going to cost extra money, and the price can really build up. Just to give you an idea of the options available:

1. Power steering, power brakes, power seats, power windows, power antennas, power sunroofs, power door locks.
2. Air conditioners.
3. AM/FM radios, stereo cassette players, front and rear speakers.
4. Appearance extras such as wheel covers, bright metal window frames, vinyl inserts on body and roof, special bumper guards, color-keyed carpets, license plate frames, fender skirts.
5. Lights, including map light, fog lights, glove box and ashtray light, trunk

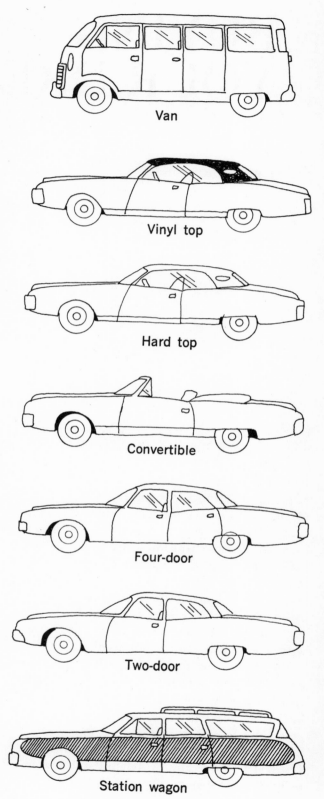

Van

Vinyl top

Hard top

Convertible

Four-door

Two-door

Station wagon

light, seat belt warning light, brake warning light, engine compartment lights.

6. Upholstery, including all vinyl, cloth and vinyl, knitted vinyl, leather.
7. Seats, including bench type, bucket type, high backs, fold down, split bench.
8. Special instruments: oil pressure gauge, tachometer, trip meter, electric clock, engine temperature gauge.
9. Special tires, as mentioned in Chapter 4.
10. Window washers.
11. Special locks, burglar alarms and devices.
12. Cartop carriers, tow bars, special heavy duty towing equipment for trailing.
13. Tinted glass.
14. Automatic transmission.

Check these against your list of standard equipment as some cars do include some of these as standard items. And, remember, this is only a partial list. Talk to your dealer, but don't be talked into anything. Choose wisely.

MONEY

This will probably be your most important consideration, so here are some ways you can pay for the new car:

1. All cash (or check).
2. Financing. After a down payment, the remainder is paid over an estimated time period.
3. An old car is turned in and either cash or financing is used for the remainder of the payment.
4. A passbook loan.

Let's take a look at each of these items more carefully.

Cash (or check). We don't have to talk much about total cash payment. Just be sure you get a proper receipt along with guarantees and warranties. Also, keep in mind that once that cash is spent, it's gone. You may not want to spend your last penny and leave yourself without financial protection. Also, if the dealer does not fulfill his obligations to you, you will have nothing to bargain with if he has received total payment for the car.

Financing. Most likely, the dealer where you buy has an arrangement for financing with a local bank, finance company, or finance associate of the manufacturer. Three of the major auto manufacturers have their own financing affiliate. But be aware that the finance company and the manufacturer's affiliate will perhaps have a higher interest rate than the bank. If you can get a better deal on your own, by all means do so. Before you sign any contract agreement, be sure you understand all the terms.

Be aware of the Truth in Lending Act, a federal law that lets the borrower check the cost of financing a car by comparing it with other loans. The lender *must* reveal the details of the contract including the exact interest rate annually for the exact specified time period.

Usually financing involves:

1. Down payment.
2. Time allotted to pay the remainder.
3. Interest percentage to be added to this remainder.
4. A schedule of payments so there are no unexpected monies due on the last payment.

Remember that the less cash down payment you make the more the car will eventually cost. It costs money to borrow money. That's what interest is all about.

Here's an example: If your car costs $3000

and you pay $500 cash, you'll have $2500 left to pay. If it must be paid within three years (36 months) and your interest is 10% annually, your monthly payments will be $80.67 for the three years, or a total of $2904.12 in addition to your $500 down payment. This is just a sample. I can't give you an exact formula for financing in these pages because of variations in local taxes, financial rates, and insurance rates. But when you talk to the dealer or bank, be sure to know exactly what your monthly payments will be *including* interest.

Many banks or dealers will give you a booklet with twelve, twenty-four, or thirty-six tear-out tabs, one tab to be sent with each monthly payment. This way you will know quickly how many monthly payments are left.

The turn (trade) in. If you have an old car, you may wish to exchange it as part payment for your new car. The dealer will often offer you "book value" for your old car. This is a pricing value established by the National Automobile Dealers Association. You may feel that the quoted book value is too low. Your dealer may also realize that the care you have given this auto makes it worth more. He may then offer you a better deal. If you are still not satisfied, you can try to sell the car on your own. But this means that *you* must advertise it, *you* must convince the potential buyer, and that *you* must do the paper work. Sometimes the inconvenience is not worth the extra money you gain by selling it on your own.

Passbook loan. If you have the cash available in your savings account, you may borrow the money for the auto from your savings account, giving the bank your passbook as collateral (guarantee) for repayment. This money may not be touched until the loan is paid back. But as you pay back the loan to the savings bank, your original money continues to earn interest. Your interest on the passbook loan (for example, 8%) minus the interest that your loan money continues to earn in the savings bank (for example, 5%) means that your loan costs you only 3% interest. You can see the advantage of this type of loan over the straight (for example, 10%) auto loan.

ADDITIONAL COSTS

You should know that in addition to the cost of financing you will also be burdened with the cost of:

1. Insurance.
2. Gas and oil.
3. Repairs and parts.
4. Garaging or parking if you have no facilities where you live.

Of course there is the added cost of depreciation. Even if you sell the car one week after purchase you will be lucky to get back the major portion of the price you paid.

YOUR NEW-USED DREAM CAR

Unless a used car comes highly recommended, it is much better to buy one from a reputable neighborhood dealer than from an individual. A dealer's cars, in most states, must meet certain required standards. But you should still request a guarantee from this dealer.

Stay close to home when shopping for a used car. If you go far afield, the dealer will know you're looking for a bargain and may try to take advantage of the distance between your home and his dealership. Don't go looking for any great bargains in a used-car lot. Dealers are professional and know the value of each car. If they're honest, they'll give you a car worth the dollars you pay. But there is always some risk in buying a used car because of its used machinery.

If you have an auto mechanic, girlfriend, cousin, brother-in-law, or grandfather whom you trust as a good mechanic with common sense, the used-car dealer should have no objection to letting that person look the car over. This is common practice. Your mechanic, of course, will expect to be recompensed for this.

To some extent you can use your own common sense when looking at a used car.

1. Look for painted patches or mismatched color fenders, doors, or other crash damage.
2. Look for worn upholstery, floor mats, and arm rests on the doors. Do they seem to indicate more wear than the mileage on the speedometer would indicate?
3. Check the tires for wear (see Chapter 4). Also, stay away from retread tires. A ridge or line of rubber around the side wall is very suspicious. It means that the old tire has had a new shell of rubber put on the surface.
4. Cast your eye over the car and look for anything that is out of alignment or misshapen, such as a lopsided bumper, a hood that slopes to one side.
5. Do not consider buying an ex-taxicab. If you suspect that one has been reconditioned into a private car, look at the dashboard for holes that may have housed a meter. Look on the roof for a stain the size of a removed taxi sign.

TEST DRIVE YOUR POTENTIAL CAR

Get in. Does the door close securely? Adjust the seat. Does it move properly? Is the visibility good all around. Adjust the mirrors.

Ask where the controls for the windshield wipers and headlights are. Try them. Try the heater and defroster.

Drive it. Does the car steer easily? Hold the wheel lightly. Does it tend to pull to one side? Check the brakes. Are they firm, and do they stop the car properly? (See braking details in Chapter 9.)

Try to incorporate both stop-and-go traffic and highway travel in your test-drive route.

For your comfort. Are the seats comfortable? Do you have enough elbow room? Are the positions of the pedals comfortable? Can you see without craning your neck?

Listen. Listen for a smooth-running engine both at idle and when moving. Listen for squeaks, squeals, and squawks. Listen for engine noise. It could mean poor interior insulation, and this would prove very annoying. Listen when you shift gears or when the transmission automatically does. Is there a bump or growl?

Feel. Feel for drafts. Feel for unusual vibrations.

Smell. Smell for exhaust fumes, gasoline fumes, heat smells, or burning rubber.

RENTING OR LEASING

Renting. If you have only occasional need for a car, then ownership is a luxury. Consider renting for that week's vacation or day-long business trip. Some insurance is included in the rental, and additional insurance is available. Also, the rental company takes the responsibility for any mechanical failure. And keep in mind that many rental companies do not require that you bring the car back to that same rental office. If you're driving from

Chicago to Springfield, Illinois, you do not have to return the car to Chicago.

But be aware that in larger cities, the car must often be reserved well in advance for a summer or holiday weekend. And be aware that some companies have more costly weekend rates.

Leasing. Many different plans are available for long-term auto leasing. Some plans include full maintenance and insurance. Costs will vary according to the locale, the individual's driving record and credit rating, and the length of the lease. There is even an arrangement whereby the cost of the leasing can be put toward the eventual purchase of the car at the end of the lease period.

The greatest advantage of leasing is to those who put a great deal of mileage and wear-and-tear on a car. You will not have to absorb the cost of depreciation on a leased car as you would with your own car.

There are many pros and cons to leasing. If you are considering it, talk to a leasing firm and find out what they have to offer. You will have to make your own decision.

The most important thing to remember when you have acquired a car is to take care of it. This responsibility is always on your shoulders if you want good value. Neglect could cost someone his life. Respect your car and don't abuse it.

14. FOR SAFETY'S SAKE

DEFENSIVE DRIVING

Defensive driving is a term I'm sure you've heard over and over. Do you consider it just a catchy line, or do you drive this way? I can't stress enough the importance of being aware of every car around you and being aware of every existing situation as well as any situation that may come up. When you see kids playing ball, do you suddenly become more alert? How about a straying pet? Or a brakelight suddenly going on far ahead in a line of traffic? Or the driver in the next lane conversing too much with a passenger to be aware of his driving? Are you aware that a car entering the parkway may cause the car at your side to change lanes? Think these are not your problems? Don't kid yourself. Do you see that "tailgater" four cars ahead? Do you know how he could affect you if he collided with the tail of the car that he's too close to? You *must* be aware of these situations on today's crowded roads.

Try to observe the following rules:

1. Drive at least one car length behind the car ahead for each ten miles per hour that you drive.

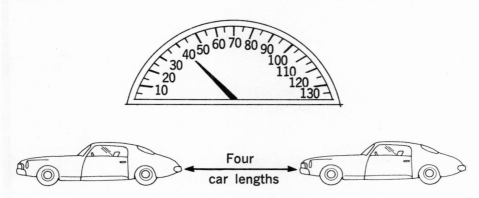

Four car lengths

2. Signal all your intended moves in advance.

3. Mentally check each scene as it happens. Use your rear-view mirror very frequently; constantly glance about at the whole picture, not just what's in front of you. Look for trouble spots and avoid them by driving sensibly.

WINTER DRIVING FOR SAFETY'S SAKE

When driving in cold or snowy weather you must become aware of circumstances that under normal conditions wouldn't cross your mind.

Driving in snow. Be sure to clean your windows thoroughly before starting off. Don't just sweep the back of your mittened hand over the windshield in a basketball-sized circle. You need to be especially concerned about visibility under snowy conditions. Also, be sure to wipe snow and ice from the headlights and taillights.

Be sure you have snow tires or chains. If you do get stuck in a snow bank, apply the accelerator gently. Spinning the wheels will only cause them to dig in deeper. Try to keep the wheels straight ahead. Turning the wheels in order to start may cause the rear of the car to spin around.

Don't violently rock the car back and forth hoping to "jackrabbit" out of the snow. This can ruin your automatic transmission. Try rolling forward a bit and then backward a bit, ever increasing the flattened track you make for yourself. If you still can't get any traction, try putting some sand or gravel or even an old raincoat in front of the rear wheels; try anything that might give them a grip in the snow. But be gentle when you press the accelerator.

Carry some wintertime equipment: a bag of sand, a windshield scraper, a small shovel, boots, heavy gloves and, of course, the standard equipment mentioned in Chapter 1—a flashlight, rags, and so on.

If you drive at night in snow, don't use your high beams. The low beams (not the parking lights) give less glare and direct their light to the edge of the road.

Be sure your windshield washer has antifreeze in its container.

And last, but certainly not least, decrease your normal driving speed.

Driving on ice. When you drive on icy roadways, always remember to drive more slowly, stop gently by lightly pumping the brakes, steer gradually and slowly, and increase greatly your distance between the car in front of you. Beware if the sun has melted the ice. The shady spots may still have a skim of ice under their melted surfaces.

Slow down at intersections and on curves.

In some areas snow tires or chains *must* be be used on certain streets. You could risk a ticket if you don't have them and you get stuck.

Skidding on ice is sometimes unavoidable and always frightening. About the only thing you can do is learn how to control the skid. The most important and the most difficult thing is to keep your wits about you.

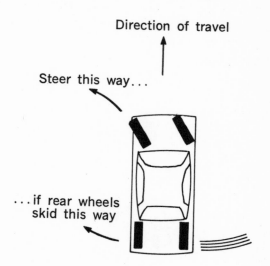

Direction of travel

Steer this way...

...if rear wheels skid this way

If you feel your car going into a skid, do *not* touch the brake immediately. That will only prolong the skid. Steer gently in the same direction that the *rear* end of the car is skidding in order to regain control.

As you feel control of direction coming back, straighten the wheel and gently pump the brake until you've gotten control.

DRIVING AT NIGHT

Headlights are perhaps the most important item in night driving. Be sure they're functioning properly and that they're clean.

Don't look directly at the headlights of oncoming traffic. Dim your bright lights for an oncoming car. This is not just a courtesy. If you don't dim them and the other driver is blinded by them, an accident could result.

Keep your windshield clean, both inside and out. A dirty or greasy windshield can distort the other lights around you.

If you have been drinking, of course, do not drive. But also beware of the big meal. A warm cozy car and a full stomach can make you very drowsy. Keep the car cool or drive with a window open, and if you feel too tired to continue, pull off the road and take a nap, or let someone else drive, if you are not alone.

DRIVING IN RAIN OR FOG

Wet pavements can be as slippery and dangerous as icy roads. An especially critical time is just at the start of the rain when the roadway becomes slightly wet and mixes with the accumulated grease and oil embedded in its porous surface. This can make the road extremely slick, so drive with added caution.

Be sure your windshield washer and wipers are in good condition. Grime and mud can be thrown onto your windshield from passing cars and interfere with the washer's function-

ing. Be sure your windshield wiper blades are in good condition.

When headlights are necessary in heavy rain or fog, use only the low beam. This will illuminate the edge of the roadway, whereas the high beam will tend to glare back at you.

DRIVING IN GOOD WEATHER

Even on a nice day you have responsibilities for safety.

Keep up with traffic. Don't become an obstacle to other drivers. This could cause other drivers to take risks trying to get around you. If they take dangerous chances because you are driving too slowly, you could become involved in their accident, and you would be partially responsible.

countryside is *all* you get as the driver, and even that can be dangerous. Do your glancing when no other cars are around.

Watch out for sun-dappled roadways or sudden changes from brilliant sunlight to deep shadow. It's a good idea to wear good-grade sunglasses. This will help lessen the contrast of the light and shadow and eliminate glare.

YOUR DISABLED VEHICLE

If your car should break down on the road, try your best to get the car off the roadway and onto the shoulder. A car with a flat can be driven slowly from a dangerous area but you will probably ruin the tire. Use your emergency warning lights or light flares to signal other drivers.

If the car is immovable and in a dangerous position, get all passengers away from it.

A white cloth fastened to the radio antenna or the door handle is a signal to the police and passing drivers that you need help.

DRIVING EMERGENCIES

Can you handle driving emergencies? The most important thing is to keep your wits about you. Keep cool. Think before you act.

If you are faced with a driving emergency, here are some possible solutions for you. They could lessen the disastrous outcome of a sudden crisis.

The loss of a wheel or a blowout. What happens to your car and what you should do about it are very similar in both incidents. Hold on tightly to the steering wheel (it will want to jar out of your hands). Steer straight ahead and let up on the gas pedal. Signal a warning to drivers behind you by lightly touching the brake pedal. Don't brake hard until you have slowed down, and even then brake gently. Ignore any terrible noises that you hear. They can be frightening.

Driving back onto the roadway. Don't try to quickly swing back up the ridge onto the pavement. This could throw the car completely off balance and even turn it over. Slow down, signal and turn back sharply onto the pavement.

Brakes fail. Try pumping the brake pedal to regain pressure. If this doesn't work, put the car into a lower gear. This will slow you down. Then start applying the emergency brake by pulling it on, releasing it, pulling it on, releasing it until the car stops. Don't yank it on and hold it because this could burn right through the brake linings until you have no brakes at all.

Steering fails. Don't tromp on the brake because the car could swerve violently. Slow down by taking your foot off the accelerator and shifting to a lower gear. As the car slows, gently apply and release the brake repeatedly.

Sticking accelerator pedal. Try putting your toe beneath the pedal and forcing it upward. If this is unsuccessful, brake gently until you slow down enough to turn off the engine. (Turning off the engine on newer cars at any speed will lock the anti-theft steering mechanism.) If nothing you do will free the pedal do not try to continue on your way. You'll need help.

Fire. If you see smoke or flames anywhere in your car, get off the road and turn off the engine. I've advised that you carry a fire extinguisher. Know how to use it! Do not try to put out the fire with water. (This might only spread it.) If the fire is beyond control, get out of the way and motion other motorists away. Then get someone to call the fire department or police.

A car is coming head on. If possible, pull to your right. If you pull left into the lane *the oncoming car should be in,* the driver could suddenly become aware of what he's doing and swerve back into his own lane. Honk your horn, blink your lights. He could be asleep.

Stranded on the railroad tracks. If you cannot push the car or have it pushed before a train comes along, abandon the car.

SAFETY EQUIPMENT

To help prevent injury, special equipment has been developed and made available.

Safety belts are one of the most effective lifesaving tools. Statistics prove this. I don't care what arguments you've heard against them. The shoulder harness is even more effective and is not less comfortable. They're standard equipment in new cars; use them.

For small tots, there are specially designed children's seats that attach to seat belts and wedge into the cushions.

There are head restraints on most newer cars that effectively reduce the neck injuries that are so common in accidents.

There are padded dashboards and also steering wheels that cushion you.

There is shatterproof glass, heavy-duty side-beam protection, and heavy bumpers.

RANDOM THOUGHTS FOR SAFETY

Keep your car free of heavy, loose objects that can fly around. Don't keep a can of oil or antifreeze or anything on the back shelf. Don't put tools or a flashlight on the dashboard. Don't let your child play with his favorite truck on the rear shelf. Try to put all purchases in the trunk.

Don't let children stand, run, jump, or skip rope in the car. They *should* sit quietly with their seat belts on, even though this is difficult to accomplish. Try to involve them in quiet games like license plate poker or at least have them count the out-of-staters.

Use your emergency blinkers if you have a breakdown.

Keep a window open a couple of inches even in winter so that you have fresh air. This could save your life if you have an undetected exhaust leak. Carbon monoxide, which is odorless, could seep into your car without your being aware of it.

Don't drive if you have been taking medication, including over-the-counter cold remedies, which might affect your ability to see or react. If you are ill, upset, or overtired, do not drive.

Be sure your car is in good condition, with all mechanisms functioning properly.

Be sure your mirrors are properly adjusted.

Be sure all your doors are locked while driving.

Never leave children and keys in the car alone together.

On a long trip, make frequent stops to avoid sleepiness.

In other words, use your good common sense!

15. IF YOU HAVE AN ACCIDENT

THE PERSON WHO drives regularly in populated areas can expect from ten to twelve bumps, jars, and fender benders throughout his driving career. Let's hope it's never more than that. However, you should be always prepared to contend with an accident.

IF YOU SEE AN ACCIDENT COMING

You can lessen possible injury if you and your passengers are wearing seat belts. If you are aware of the coming impact, place your hands on the upper part of the steering wheel (your front seat passenger should place hands on the dashboard), lean forward and rest your forehead on the backs of your hands. If you are wearing the more effective shoulder harness, press your body forward against it and bend your head forward with hands against the steering wheel.

AFTER THE IMPACT

Assuming you are able, stop the car, turn off the ignition, and move away from the car. Do *not* leave the scene. You are legally bound to this responsibility. Put out any cigarettes; there could be spilled gasoline in the area.

If your accident is minor and there are no tempers flaring and there is no need for the police, give the other driver only the following information:

1. Your name.
2. Your address.
3. Your driver's license number.
4. Your vehicle registration number.
5. Your license plate number.
6. The name of your insurance company and your policy number.

(You should have a pencil and paper in the car at all times.)

Ask him for the same information and write it down. If he refuses to give it to you, write down his license plate number and report it along with what happened to the police.

If the other driver does become abusive, do *not* become so yourself. Ask someone for police assistance. Right or wrong, do *not* make any statements to anyone as to fault.

You should be the only spokesman for your car. Never let a child make any statement. He may start talking about an incident that occurred three days earlier. And your Aunt Elsie may mean well but keep her quiet! Gag her if necessary.

Even if the other driver admits all fault and promises to make all repairs, take the steps noted in this chapter. This driver could magically disappear when the bills come in.

Do not tell anyone how much insurance coverage you have.

Do not tell anyone but the police and your insurance agent the names of the witnesses.

If the other driver has been drinking, demand that a chemical test be given to both this driver *and* yourself.

The police should be notified if:

1. There is an injury.
2. There is extensive damage.
3. Tempers flare.

Give the police the precise location of the accident. Let them know if there are any injuries and if they seem serious enough to warrant an ambulance. If you're not sure, request one anyway.

If the other car drives away, try to get his license number or at least a portion of it. Try to get a description of the car: color, make, type, year.

AID TO THE INJURED

If an accident is serious, the first responsibility of those able is aid to the injured.

If you know nothing about first aid, do nothing for a person's injury. Moving him, for instance, could cause more serious injury. Think only of his comfort; a blanket for shock or warmth, a gentle cushioning under his head. But you *should* know some basic first aid. For instance, if there is excessive bleeding externally, you should know how to locate the pressure points in order to stem the flow of blood.

After the victim has been laid down, to stop the bleeding press a sterile gauze dressing over the wound and apply pressure, using your whole hand.

Lay a fresh gauze over the wound if the first one becomes soaked with blood, continuing the pressure.

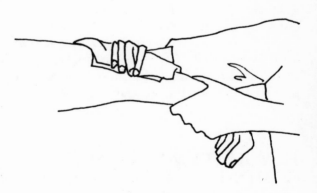

If the bleeding cannot be stopped by this method, try shutting the circulation from the artery by pressing firmly on it with your palm. Learn and remember the four basic pressure points where artery pressure is effective. Do not try arterial pressure for wounds to the head, neck, or torso.

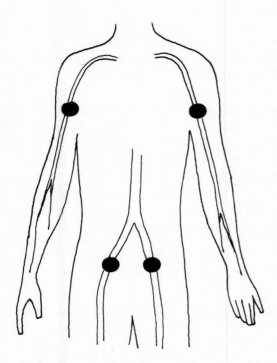

Shock. If a person has gone into shock, he will become pale, cold, and clammy. His breathing will be shallow and fast, and his pulse rapid.

Have the victim lie down with his feet elevated slightly. (If he has a chest or head wound, raise his head instead. Only if he develops breathing difficulties should you lower his head.)

Keep him warm, but do not overheat him.

Burns. If a person is badly burned, have him lie down to avoid shock. Do *not* apply any oils, ointments, or antiseptics. If possible, cover the victim with a very clean cloth; perhaps a freshly laundered sheet from a nearby home. This is done to exclude contaminating air, since burns are highly susceptible to infection.

Head injury. After a bad rap on the head, the victim will be dazed or unconscious. He may have bleeding from the mouth, ears, or nose. He may experience dizziness, rapid pulse, or headache.

Keep him lying down and warm until the ambulance comes. Lying quietly lessens the chance of brain hemorrhage.

If he is bleeding from the mouth turn his head sideways so blood can drain from his mouth. If the head is bleeding, gently place a sterile bandage on the wound. Do not apply pressure. Stay with him to keep movement at a minimum. Do *not* give him any stimulants.

A NON-COLLISION ACCIDENT

Carbon monoxide poisoning. This lethal gas is odorless and colorless. However, carbon monoxide is contained in the exhaust fumes from the running engine, and these you can smell. Thus it is important not to breathe in car exhaust for any prolonged period of time.

The person overcome by carbon monoxide will be dizzy, have difficulty breathing, and may have vomiting spells. Continued exposure to this poison for even a short time produces unconsciousness and death. So get the victim into fresh air quickly and use mouth to mouth resuscitation if the victim

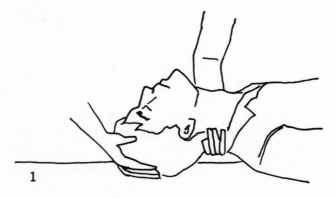

1

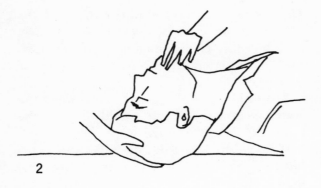

2

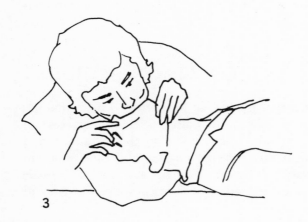

3

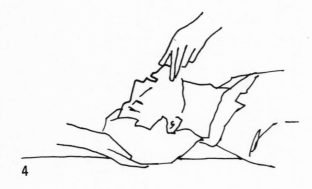

4

is not breathing. After calling the police or fire department, have him lie quietly and keep him comfortable. Specify in your call for help that there has been carbon monoxide poisoning so that proper equipment will be supplied.

REPORTING YOUR ACCIDENT

As soon as you can, notify your insurance company of the accident. If the accident happens far from home, notify your company's nearest claim office. If you cannot physically report it, ask either the police or the hospital to do so.

While it is fresh in your mind and as soon as you have a quiet moment, reconstruct the details of the accident on paper. Try to draw a diagram of the scene of the accident.

You may have to report the accident to the proper state bureau. Check with the police department or your insurance agent to see if this is necessary.

YOUR CAR

If your car is being towed away, find out its destination. After the first frenzy of activity caused by the accident subsides, find out the storage costs for the car. It may be sitting for a few days while you arrange for repairs.

Your insurance company will usually send an adjustor who will estimate the cost of the necessary repairs. If you cannot find a shop that will do the repairs for that price, it is up to the insurance company to find one. The insurance company then pays the bill.

LEGAL AFTERMATHS

If you receive any communication regarding the accident or any letter from a lawyer representing the other driver, turn this information over immediately to your insurance agent.

If, after a serious accident, an insurance adjustor arrives with a tape recorder or a barrage of questions, ask him to submit the questions in writing. Do not let him confuse you. If you retain a lawyer, do not sign anything without his knowledge. Remember that the insurance adjustor looks after his company's interests (which is an excellent reason to retain a lawyer yourself; he or she will represent *you*).

When you can collect under the other owner's insurance coverage for your damaged property, it is advisable to do so as quickly as possible.

Personal injury is another problem. An injury may not be evident for three or four months. Don't sign a release on personal injury responsibility (liability) until you're sure all injuries are known. The insurance company should, in the meantime, pay for hospital costs, equipment used, and drug expense. There should also be an allowance for pain and suffering. However, this is controversial, different for each case, and difficult to determine; you'll want a lawyer's services.

If there is permanent injury, especially to the family breadwinner, estimates become more complicated.

If a satisfactory conclusion is not reached, it may be necessary to file suit. You should secure a lawyer and follow his advice.

INSURANCE-POLICY TERMINOLOGY

Liability. This does not cover damage to your car or injury to you and your passengers. It covers those you injure and any property that you damage other than your own car. For your protection, it pays for any bodily injury or any property damage for which you are held responsible. This includes a neighbor's lamppost, a pedestrian you may hit, a supermarket basket you may drive over or an auto with which you may collide. You are held responsible for your action. Your insurance company will handle the complaint (or claim) and pay the damage settlement up to the amount for which you are insured.

Collision. This covers damage to *your* car even if the accident is your fault. If your car is fairly new, it might be wise to have this in addition to liability.

Fifty-dollar deductible—The insurance company will pay for any damage over $50. You must pay the first $50.

One-hundred-dollar deductible—The company will pay anything over $100. You must pay the first $100.

Various options like this are available.

Comprehensive. This will pay for damage to your car as a result of fire, storm, theft, or vandalism. This policy is also available with deductibles.

Medical. This protects you and your passengers against medical and hospital expenses that result from an automobile accident. It also protects you as a pedestrian if you are injured by a car.

If you have medical policies through another source that give you this protection, you may choose to limit or eliminate this coverage.

Bodily injury liability. This protects you if your car should injure or kill others. If you are held responsible, this policy includes bail bond expenses, court costs, and financial compensation to the party who has suffered the loss.

Uninsured motorist insurance. This protects you if you or your passengers suffer bodily injury or death due to an uninsured or a hit-and-run driver.

Assigned risk insurance. If a person is often involved in accidents he is considered a high- (assigned-) risk driver. Most insurance companies want to avoid insuring these people. Special insurance plans are available for just such people. However, the rate of payment for coverage is much greater than for a safe driver.

No-fault insurance. Some state laws have changed to require that you carry auto insurance using the "no-fault" system. This means that you may recover compensation promptly from your own company whoever is to blame. The theory is that excessively high insurance costs will drop and the courts will be free of costly, time-consuming decisions as to who is at fault. It is a very controversial subject. If your state is considering adopting no-fault insurance, read all you can concerning it and come to your own conclusion.

HOW MUCH INSURANCE?

How much insurance you have and how much you pay depends on a number of factors.

1. Your age.
2. Your driving record.
3. The make and model of your car (high-powered racing car or modest subcompact).
4. Special equipment you may use (trailer, plow, etc.).
5. Whether you use your car for business.
6. How many drive the car; who and how old they are.
7. Where you live (flood, extreme cold, high-risk, theft, and vandalism areas).

The amount of insurance necessary depends on the assets you have. What must you protect? A house? Property? A business? Think of what can be taken from you if the worst thing happens—you cause another person's death. Be sure to protect yourself and your family from financial ruin.

A popular consumer magazine has published the following handy accident report card. Tear it out and keep it in your glove compartment. In fact, some of the information can be filled in right now. Do so. It could help in case of an accident, or even illness, on the road.

IN CASE OF ACCIDENT

I. Fill in now and retain.

Phone number of my local hospital or ambulance service _____

   my physician _____   my local garage _____

   tow service _____   auto club _____

My Social Security No. _____

My Accident and Health Policy No. _____

II. Information to give to other driver (tear on dotted lines):

Car Owner _____

Street _____ City _____ State _____ ZIP _____

Car Driver _____

Street _____ City _____ State _____ ZIP _____

Driver's License No. _____ State _____

Driver's Date of Birth: Month _____ Day _____ Year _____

Make of Car _____ Color _____ Model _____ Year _____

Insurance Co. _____ Policy No. _____

Registration Plates _____ State _____

III. Information to get for your insurance company (and see over):

Other Car's Owner _____

Street _____ City _____ State _____ ZIP _____

Other Car's Driver _____

Street _____ City _____ State _____ ZIP _____

Driver's Date of Birth: Month _____ Day _____ Year _____

Driver's License _____ State _____ Expires 19 _____

License Plates _____ State _____ Expires 19 _____

Make of car _____ Color _____ Model _____ Year _____

Insurance Co. _____ Policy No. _____

Scene of Accident: State _____ City _____ Street or Rte. _____

Date of Accident: Month _____ Year: 19 _____ at _____A.M. _____P.M.

Weather: Clear _____ Rain _____ Snow _____ Fog _____

Road Condition: Dry _____ Wet _____ Icy _____ Sanded _____

Damage to Other Car Includes: _____

Adapted from Family Circle Car Card by Nan Findlow
© 1972 by **Family Circle.** Reprinted by permission.

Information to get for your insurance company (continued):

Damage to My Car Includes: _____

_____

_____

Personal Injury in My Car to: Name _____

Street _____ City _____ State _____ ZIP _____

Personal Injury in My Car to: Name _____

Street _____ City _____ State _____ ZIP _____

Personal Injury in Other Car to: Name _____

Street _____ City _____ State _____ ZIP _____

Personal Injury in Other Car to: Name _____

Street _____ City _____ State _____ ZIP _____

Witnesses Including Police Dept. (Note precinct number or location of station):

Name _____

Street _____ City _____ State _____ ZIP _____

Name _____

Street _____ City _____ State _____ ZIP _____

16. SOME DRIVING TIPS

FOR MORE ECONOMICAL DRIVING

Oil and gasoline. Be sure to buy the kind of gasoline best suited for your car. Consult your auto manual.

Be sure the engine is properly tuned. This is very important. You could be using from 10% to 20% more fuel with an improperly tuned engine.

On turnpike or country driving keep your speedometer at a steady pace with the flow of traffic. If you drive a steady 50 miles per hour, you use a lot less gas than when driving 40, then 60, then 35, then 55 miles per hour. Keep up your speed when going uphill, and don't let it increase when going down.

Avoid unnecessary, sudden, superfast acceleration when passing.

Don't race from one red light to the next. Fast deceleration uses as much fuel as sudden acceleration.

Make sure your automatic transmission is working efficiently. If the car runs too long in low gear before shifting up, additional fuel is used.

If you tow a trailer, slow down. Don't make your car labor excessively and less gas will be used.

Change your oil and oil filter as recommended. Be sure oil level is not below its minimum (see Chapter 8 on how to check this).

Brakes. Try not to hold the brake pedal down for a continued period. Pumping, or applying short periods of pressure, will help save brake linings.

Don't ride with your foot resting on the brake pedal.

Try to avoid constant, heavy, sharp braking.

97

Tires. Be sure that tires are inflated to the pressure recommended in your manual.

Avoid screech-away starts. Those long black rubber marks on the roadway cost a couple of cents per foot in tire wear.

Slow down when turning corners. Racing around them is unsafe and it costs money. Squealing on a turn places great stress on your tires.

Drive slowly over roads where there is construction.

Have your front wheels aligned and checked periodically.

Again, avoid using the brakes heavily. It's hard on tires.

Look at the tire treads occasionally. Dig out pebbles, pieces of glass and metal.

Automatic transmission. Put your automatic transmission in low when laboring up a steep hill or when driving slowly through snow or mud. This puts less strain on the car and at the same time gives you more traction.

Manual transmission. Keep your foot off the clutch unless shifting gears. Never ride with your foot on the clutch, even if it's only slightly depressed.

Shift gears as the car slows down. Don't let the car lug along in high gear at low speeds. It makes the transmission and engine work too hard and causes wear.

Never try to start up in second gear. This puts a great strain on both the engine and transmission.

Shift to a lower gear when climbing a steep hill.

Shift to a lower gear and go down a steep hill slowly. This helps hold the car back, and you'll have less need for heavy brake pressure.

Body care. Cleanliness is one of the biggest deterrents to rust and body deterioration. Keep the car as clean as possible and protect it well with wax (see Chapter 2).

DRIVING HINTS

Parking. If you park on an uphill grade and the street has curbing, turn your wheels away from the curb.

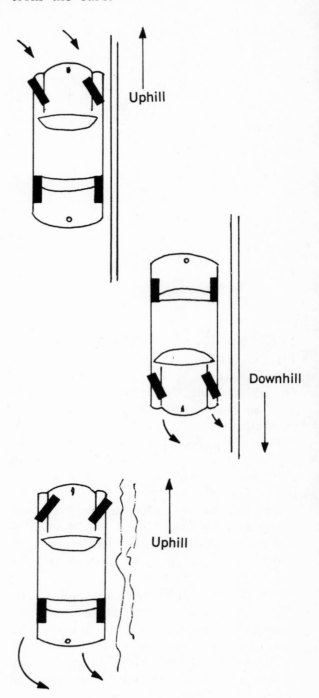

Then, if you are bumped or if your brake doesn't hold, your car will not roll backward down the hill.

However, contrary to the above instructions, if you park on an *uphill* grade with no curb, turn your wheels *toward* the *edge* of the roadway. If you roll you will want to roll *off* the road.

If you park on a downhill grade, turn your wheels toward the curb. Again, your car will roll if bumped, but only forward to the curb.

Even if there is no curbing on the *downhill* grade, follow these wheel-turning instructions so that if the car rolls it will not be into the path of traffic but off the roadway.

Never park your car and swing the door on the driver's side open without first checking for traffic.

Lock your ignition if you can when you leave the car, and lock your doors. Do this especially at night when parked on the street or in a lot. Aside from the possibility of theft, anyone could get in and hide in the back of the car.

ROAD SIGNS

The United States is gradually converting to a standardized marking system for all states. Here's what a few of the new signs will look like.

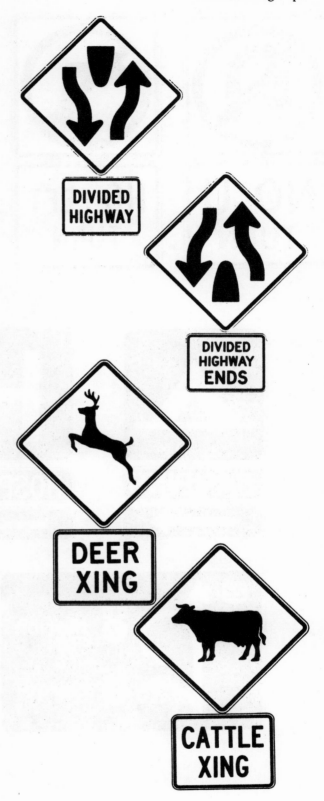

You may have already seen these signs in your area. If not, you should see them in the near future.

17. TROUBLE CHART

TROUBLE	SOME POSSIBLE REASONS
IGNITION AND FUEL PROBLEMS	
Engine turns over but will not start	1. Out of gasoline 2. Defective fuel pump 3. Clogged fuel filter or fuel line 4. Carburetor float valve stuck 5. Damp spark plugs, coil, or distributor cap 6. Not enough spark (weak coil) 7. High-tension wires loose or wet
Starter won't turn engine over	1. Ignition switch malfunctioning 2. Dead battery 3. Battery connections loose or corroded 4. Starter connections loose

TROUBLE	SOME POSSIBLE REASONS
Engine runs raggedly	1. Automatic choke needs adjusting 2. Water or dirt in gasoline 3. Fuel pump functioning badly 4. Engine needs service and tuning adjustment 5. Improper fuel being used
Engine backfires	1. Too lean a gasoline mixture (often because water or dirt is in fuel) 2. Engine too cold with too little choke 3. Sticking intake valve 4. Broken valve spring 5. Spark plug wires not in proper sequence 6. Distributor cap cracked

ALTERNATOR PROBLEMS

TROUBLE	SOME POSSIBLE REASONS
Alternator does not charge	1. Fan (or drive) belt slips, or belt is not the proper tautness 2. Faulty connections on output terminal 3. Alternator brushes sticking
Noisy alternator	1. Fan belt or drive belt out of alignment or loose 2. Bearings worn
Rate of charging unsteady	1. Connections loose 2. Fan (or drive) belt loose or slipping 3. Bad connections or corrosion on battery terminals

TROUBLE	SOME POSSIBLE REASONS
COOLING SYSTEM	
Water-cooled engine overheats. Cooling not functioning	1. Fan belt slips 2. Radiator needs water 3. Water circulation sluggish (because of rust, dirt, etc. in the cooling system) 4. Thermostat malfunctions 5. Water hoses rotted 6. Outside of radiator clogged with bugs, leaves, etc. 7. Water pump malfunctions 8. Hose connections loose
Air-cooled engine overheats	1. Fan belt broken or slipping 2. Blower bearing worn 3. Damper doors jammed or out of line 4. Cooling fins clogged with bugs, leaves, dirt 5. Thermostat malfunctioning
OIL SYSTEM PROBLEMS	
Engine oil leaks	1. Oil pan drain plug loose 2. Crack or break in oil pan 3. Gaskets leak 4. Oil-seal leaks 5. An oil passage clogged 6. Oil filter leaks
Oil consumption high	1. Oil leaks 2. Worn piston rings or cylinder walls 3. Worn pistons and cylinders 4. Worn main bearings

TROUBLE	SOME POSSIBLE REASONS
No oil pressure	1. Defective light in oil-pressure warning signal on dashboard 2. Crankcase in need of oil 3. Oil pump broken 4. Oil passages or screen clogged 5. Pressure relief valve stuck in open position

BRAKE PROBLEMS

Brakes won't engage	1. Not enough brake fluid, or fluid is dirty 2. Brake linings worn 3. Air in hydraulic system 4. Master cylinder malfunctioning 5. Wheel cylinders malfunctioning
Car pulls to one side	1. Brake drum not round in shape 2. Tires not properly inflated 3. Brake shoe badly adjusted or worn 4. Front suspension worn 5. Oil or grease on brake material 6. Wheel cylinders malfunctioning
Brake pedal hard. Needs excessive pressure to affect	1. Brake line not passing fluid through it properly 2. Brake shoes out of adjustment 3. Brake linings worn 4. Oil or grease in lining
Brake pedal spongy	1. Fluid leaking 2. Air in system

TROUBLE	SOME POSSIBLE REASONS
AUTOMATIC TRANSMISSION	
Car won't move in gear	1. Transmission fluid low 2. Gear selector mechanism worn or out of adjustment 3. Parking brake on 4. Universal joint broken 5. Mechanism inside transmission broken
Shifting gears rough or nonexistent	1. Transmission fluid low 2. Linkage between carburetor and transmission malfunctioning 3. Gear selector linkage broken 4. Mechanism inside transmission broken
Transmission fluid leaking	1. Loose drain plug 2. Defective sealing gaskets 3. Fluid level too high 4. Cracked transmission case
Gear won't move out of park	1. Gear selector mechanism out of adjustment 2. Parking parts damaged inside transmission 3. Broken or loose motor mounts
MANUAL TRANSMISSION	
Jumps out of gear	1. Worn or maladjusted shift linkage 2. Worn clutch gear teeth on drive gear 3. Transmission loose or out of line 4. Play or looseness in main drive gear

TROUBLE	SOME POSSIBLE REASONS
Sticks in gear	1. Clutch not releasing properly 2. Rusted transmission lever 3. Malfunction of synchronizer sleeve 4. Lack of lubrication
Difficult shifting	1. Clutch out of adjustment 2. Lack of lubricant 3. Worn shift linkage 4. Clutch pedal not being pressed fully 5. Defective synchronizer unit 6. Burned-out or damaged clutch-release bearing 7. Gearshift selector linkage worn
Noisy in gear	1. Lack of lubricant 2. Synchronizers worn 3. Transmission loose or out of line 4. Main drive gear worn or damaged 5. Reverse gear worn, or idler gear or shaft worn
CLUTCH	
Clutch chatters	1. Worn clutch bearings 2. Loose engine mounts 3. Clutch damp or wet 4. Clutch surfaces oily
Clutch slips (clutch plate will not hold tightly against face of flywheel)	1. Worn clutch pressure springs 2. Riding with foot on clutch pedal 3. Lack of lubrication 4. Worn clutch facings

TROUBLE	SOME POSSIBLE REASONS
BATTERY PROBLEMS	
Needs recharge frequently	1. Defective alternator 2. Voltage regulator contacts corroded 3. Voltage regulator set incorrectly 4. Corroded battery cables 5. Loose contacts or grounds on ignition circuits 6. Voltage regulator fuse blown
WHEEL PROBLEMS	
Noise from a particular wheel as it rotates	1. Pebble(s) in tire tread 2. Paper, tree branch, or leaves jammed in fender well are brushing against tire 3. Loose item in hubcap 4. Wheel bearing worn 5. Loose brake shoes
EXHAUST PROBLEMS	
Noisy exhaust system	1. Worn, corroded, or bent muffler or exhaust pipes 2. Wrong size muffler 3. Damaged exhaust manifold gasket 4. Damaged head gasket (between cylinder head and engine block)
Exhaust fumes leaking into passenger compartment	1. Holes in floorboards 2. Holes in trunk 3. Exhaust manifold gasket damaged 4. Exhaust manifold cracked 5. Hole in muffler, tailpipe, exhaust pipe
Exhaust smokes badly from tailpipe	1. Too-rich fuel mixture from carburetor 2. Choke sticks open 3. Too much oil consumption

Index